ENERGIZING
TEACHER EDUCATION AND
PROFESSIONAL DEVELOPMENT WITH
PROBLEM-BASED
LEARNING

EDITED BY BARBARA B. LEVIN

 ASSOCIATION FOR SUPERVISION AND CURRICULUM DEVELOPMENT   ALEXANDRIA, VIRGINIA   USA

®

Association for Supervision and Curriculum Development
1703 N. Beauregard St. • Alexandria, VA 22311-1714 USA
Telephone: 1-800-933-2723 or 703-578-9600 • Fax: 703-575-5400
Web site: http://www.ascd.org • E-mail: member@ascd.org

ASCD publications present a variety of viewpoints. The views expressed or implied in this book should not be interpreted as official positions of the Association.

Printed in the United States of America.

ASCD Product No. 101002   s4/2001
ASCD member price: $19.95   nonmember price: $23.95

Library of Congress Cataloging-in-Publication Data
Energizing teacher education and professional development with problem-based learning / [edited by] Barbara B. Levin.
　　　p. cm.
Includes bibliographical references and index.
"ASCD product no. 101002"—T.p. verso.
　　ISBN 0-87120-508-4 (alk. paper)
　　1. Problem-based learning—United States—Case studies.   2. Teachers—Training of—United States—Case studies.   I. Levin, Barbara B.
　　LB1027.42 .E54   2001
　　　378'.0071—dc21   2001000176

Energizing Teacher Education and Professional Development with Problem-Based Learning

List of Figures

Acknowledgments

First and foremost, I would like to thank all the authors who wrote chapters for this book. Their contributions make it a much better resource than anything I could have written on my own. I would also like to thank Nancy Modrak at ASCD for her initial interest in this project and for providing the services of two wonderful editors whose advice and expertise were invaluable: Mark Goldberg and Margaret Oosterman. Finally, I would like to thank my husband, David Brown, for his continued love and support, and I would like to dedicate this book in memory of my father, Robert Barry, who taught me to value education and to never give up!

Introduction

BARBARA B. LEVIN

TO MEET THE GOAL OF EDUCATING BEGINNING AND EXPERIENCED TEACH-
ers for 21st century schools, those of us who work as teacher educators must use active forms of pedagogy that match the needs of
the adult learners in front of us. If we are to engage and retain the
teachers we are preparing for U.S. schools, we must continually
seek better ways to strengthen the knowledge, skills, and dispositions that they will need to be successful in diverse classrooms.
Problem-based learning (PBL) is one tool designed to foster the
kinds of active learning experiences that prospective teachers
should be engaged in during their initial teacher preparation and
that veteran teachers should experience throughout their professional lives.

What Is Problem-Based Learning (PBL)?

PBL is an instructional method that encourages learners to
apply critical thinking, problem-solving skills, and content knowledge to real-world problems and issues. Instruction is more student
centered and less teacher directed than in traditional classrooms.
Students assume considerable responsibility for their own learning
by locating much of the information they need to solve the problems
at hand. Learning is active rather than passive, integrated rather
than fragmented, cumulative rather than isolated, and connected

rather than disjointed. PBL is likely to include discussion, reflection, research, projects, and presentations. The instructor plays several roles, including lecturer, facilitator, foil, coach, and assessor. These roles entail offering guidance, instruction, and resources to help students acquire content knowledge and problem-solving skills. Evaluation is authentic, performance based, and ongoing.

PBL starts with an issue, case, or ill-structured problem that can be researched, studied, or even "solved." "Solutions," however, do not have one correct answer. Instead, many solution paths and several good answers may be possible. Different problem-solving techniques can be applied to the initial problem, and groups or individuals generally arrive at a reasonable or possible solution. Using PBL for teacher education and professional development, as presented in this book, comes in many forms, but in all cases it offers teachers opportunities to work together to solve complex problems and dilemmas related to students, teaching, learning, curriculum, and instruction.

Theoretical Rationale for PBL

Problem-based learning was originally used in the education of medical doctors in the hope that it would increase self-directed learning and improve their problem-solving skills (Barrows, 1983). It has also been applied in several disciplines in colleges and universities (Bridges, 1992; Camp, 1996) and in teaching most subjects in K–12 schools (Delisle, 1997; Stepien, Gallagher, & Workman, 1993; Torp & Sage, 1998). PBL has spread to other professions because it was found to foster growth in many areas:

- Ability to be critical thinkers.
- Skills to analyze and solve complex, real-world problems.
- Expertise in finding, evaluating, and using information resources.
- Ability to work cooperatively in groups.
- Skills to communicate orally and in written form.
- Interest in being lifelong learners and role models for students.

Problem-based learning is a good match for adult learning (Camp, 1996): It provides teachers with a variety of learning opportunities, acknowledges their personal beliefs and experiences, and expands their knowledge and skills as they engage in learning more about a problem from a multitude of perspectives. PBL is typically conducted in groups, allowing adults to work together, share their expertise, and learn from each other.

PBL is consistent with constructivist theories of learning that serve as foundations for many teacher education programs (Brooks & Brooks, 1999; Delisle, 1997; Fosnot, 1995). Teaching from a constructivist perspective, according to Brooks and Brooks (1999), means that we need to ask one big question; provide learners with time to think; and guide them to, not give them, the resources needed to answer the question. Constructivist learning is active learning and begins by eliciting and acknowledging what learners already know and believe about the task at hand. PBL, in whatever form it takes, includes all these features and honors adult learners and constructivist beliefs about learning.

Purpose of the Book

The purpose of this book is to provide a variety of field-tested examples that use PBL for teacher education in many professional development settings. The book describes PBL activities for pre-service, novice, and experienced educators at the undergraduate and graduate levels and in K–12 education. We include PBL units that can be used in a broad range of arenas—from courses on introductory education, educational psychology (and other foundations studies), and content area methods, to seminars used in field experiences, to offerings for schoolwide and districtwide staff development. Teacher educators in higher education, those who offer alternative licensure programs, and personnel responsible for the ongoing professional development of teachers in their schools and districts will find this book helpful.

We believe that if teachers are to use PBL effectively with their K–12 students, they need to personally engage in PBL at the preservice and inservice levels. Both prospective and experienced teachers need to tackle authentic problems that require *them* to find, evaluate, and use appropriate learning resources, just as they expect their students to do when the teachers engage students in PBL.

Teachers also need to experience the challenges of working together effectively in groups, so they can use group work in their own classrooms. PBL provides genuine tasks for teachers to practice their oral and written communication skills—again, tasks that are similar to what teachers will engage students in.

Format for the Book

Teacher educators author each chapter in this book and describe their experiences in using PBL in their particular professional development setting. To help readers see commonalities and differences in approaches, we use the same main headings in the seven chapters:

- Context for PBL.
- Purposes for using PBL.
- Description of the PBL assignment.
- Instructor's role.
- Assessment.
- Outcomes.
- Problems.
- Suggestions and conclusions.

Each chapter is based on actual PBL units and activities that the authors developed and taught in teacher education and professional programs throughout the United States. We encourage our readers to use the PBL activities, adapting them to meet the needs of their own students.

Chapters 1–5 offer examples of how PBL can be used with teacher education majors in colleges and universities. Although these PBL experiences were central features in courses ranging from introductory to advanced in teacher education programs at the undergraduate or graduate levels, the ideas can easily be adapted to other professional development settings for inservice teachers.

In Chapter 1, Carol Dean, from Samford University in Birmingham, Alabama, explains how she applied PBL in a foundations of education course typically taken by college sophomores exploring teaching as a profession. She used PBL to raise issues that prospective teachers must face, such as teaching diverse populations of students, funding schools, and dealing with whether or not teaching is recognized as a true profession.

In Chapter 2, Lee Shumow, from Northern Illinois University in DeKalb, Illinois, describes four PBL problems she used in her introductory educational psychology course. While learning required course content, undergraduate teacher-candidates grappled with problematic situations that they may encounter at the elementary school level.

Chapter 3, by Jean Pierce and Herbert Lange, also from Northern Illinois University, shows how they used PBL in their educational psychology learning theory course for undergraduates. To connect their students to real classrooms, a videotape of a real classroom served as the foundation for a basic problem these prospective teachers tackled: How do you address and provide for the learning needs of all children in a public school classroom?

In Chapter 4, Kate Hibbard, Barbara Levin, and Tracy Rock present a PBL unit they designed and used with undergraduate elementary education majors at the University of North Carolina at Greensboro. Its purpose was to help them acquire the knowledge, skills, and dispositions needed to work effectively with students having various disabilities in regular education classrooms.

In Chapter 5, Barbara Levin, also from the University of North Carolina at Greensboro, explains how graduate-level students worked in small, self-selected groups to design a charter school. The overall goal of this PBL project was to engage preservice teachers in a process that would help them think deeply about all facets of the elementary school curriculum, including student learning, best teaching practices, and such aspects of schooling as governance and organization, student assessment, parental involvement, school budgets, and facilities management.

Chapters 6 and 7 offer examples of how the authors, working with experienced teachers, used PBL in inservice and staff development settings. In Chapter 6, Sara Sage, from Indiana University at South Bend, describes a one-week PBL course she taught during summer school to a variety of professional educators. Sage engaged her students in solving a real, local-issue problem to teach them the components of PBL. Chapter 7, from Gwynn Mettetal of Indiana University at South Bend, discusses how classroom action research (CAR) and problem-based learning (PBL) are alike and different and describes a long-term staff development project that two Indiana districts used to support teacher inquiry in classrooms and schools. Both PBL and CAR help teachers pose and then study their own questions about their practices.

Chapter 8, the final chapter, offers answers to many frequently asked questions (FAQs) about PBL. It captures the wisdom we have gained by experimenting with and learning to use PBL effectively with preservice and inservice teachers.

For readers who would like to learn more about PBL, we list helpful References and Additional Resources at the end of the chapters. These listings are annotated to briefly describe the information you can expect to find.

References

Barrows, H. S. (1983). Problem-based, self-directed learning. *The Journal of the American Medical Association, 250,* 3077–3080.

    An article succinctly describing the educational objectives, delivery structure, and design principles of PBL. Barrows applies principles of cognitive psychology and research to the problem-solving skills of physicians to improve the delivery of the curricula in medical schools.

Bridges, E. M. (1992). *Problem-based learning for administrators.* Eugene, OR: University of Oregon (ERIC Clearinghouse on Educational Management).

    A book detailing examples of how and why PBL is used to educate school administrators.

Brooks, M. G., & Brooks, J. G. (1999). *In search of understanding: The case for constructivist classrooms* (2nd ed.). Alexandria, VA: Association for Supervision and Curriculum Development.

    A book outlining the basis for creating classrooms based on constructivist theories of learning.

Camp, G. (1996). Problem-based learning: A paradigm shift or a passing fad? *Medical Education Online, 1*(2). Available: http://www.med-ed-online.org (2000, November 30).

    A short paper summarizing some implications of recent research in PBL.

Delisle, R. (1997). *How to use problem-based learning in the classroom.* Alexandria, VA: Association for Supervision and Curriculum Development.

    A practical book explaining how to undertake PBL. It provides several examples of PBL units that can be used in K–12 settings.

Fosnot, C. T. (1995). *Constructivism.* New York: Teachers College Press.

    A book providing information about the theory, research, and practice called constructivism.

Stepien, W. J., Gallagher, S. A., & Workman, D. (1993). Problem-based learning for traditional and interdisciplinary classrooms. *Journal for the Education of the Gifted, 16*(4), 338–357.

    A research article describing successful PBL activities in two secondary education courses.

Torp, L., & Sage, S. (1998). *Problems as possibilities: Problem-based learning for K–12 education.* Alexandria, VA: Association for Supervision and Curriculum Development.

    A book explaining reasons that PBL works with students. It provides several examples of PBL in K–12 settings.

Additional Resource

Association for Supervision and Curriculum Development (ASCD). (n.d.). [Web site]. Alexandria, VA: ASCD. Available: http://www.ascd.org (2000, October 2).

    ASCD's Web site, which provides an online study guide for this book and additional information on PBL.

1 They Expect Teachers to Do That? Helping Teachers Explore and Take Ownership of Their Profession

CAROL D. DEAN

COLLEGE STUDENTS OFTEN ENTER SAMFORD UNIVERSITY WITH LITTLE understanding of the political and sociological contexts of education. When I ask students in my foundations course what the source of funding for public schools is, the typical answer is, "from the government." When I probe with, "which government?" and "in what way?" I am met with blank stares. At age 18 or 19, most college students have never considered these and other fundamental educational issues. I want my students, who are about to enter the most important profession in U.S. society, to wonder about these questions and to care about the answers.

Context for PBL

Almost all undergraduate teacher education programs have a course called Introduction to Education, Foundations of Education, or—as this course has been renamed—Issues in Education. It is typically placed early in a teacher education curriculum. At Samford University, students take it during their sophomore year, before applying for admission into the teacher education program.

The seven-week course spans a two-hour block on Mondays, Wednesdays, and Fridays during the second half of a semester. In the same block during the first half of the semester, students work in local urban schools as teacher aides. Because this is an exploratory course, a common class size is 40–60 students. The two-hour block is advantageous for PBL work, allowing students time to work together on their problems. But the limited number of classes—21—challenges me to make thoughtful selections about the most significant issues to address and to design problems that will engage students in these issues.

As a starting point for the PBL unit, I gave students, along with their problem, news articles and editorials from local newspapers and national newsmagazines. Working in groups, they were challenged to carefully research the issues presented and to draw conclusions from the facts and opinions found in both popular and professional literature. I contacted eight school administrators in the community and asked them to serve as mentors and to provide students with a context for the issues. I sent the administrators a copy of the problem and a list of learning issues that I hoped would emerge. Each group was assigned a mentor to visit and interview about their group's specific problem. The mentor often set up classroom observations to broaden students' understanding of the problem.

Purposes for Using PBL

In traditional foundations courses, students explore the historical and philosophical background of the modern educational system in the United States, with the expectation that this knowledge will provide a base for understanding current issues and teaching methodologies. Questions from foundations courses are prominent on many teacher examinations, such as those in The Praxis Series: Professional Assessments for Beginning Teachers®. Outside their concern about what facts to memorize for the exam, however, students in Samford's program rarely view this course as important for their preparation to become a teacher. Furthermore, many college students take little time to read a newspaper or watch the local news, so undergraduates are often unaware of the issues surrounding education.

The course was redesigned, using PBL in an effort to make historical, philosophical, and current issues more relevant and engaging for these future teachers—to help them view their chosen field as a true profession worthy of their intellect and passion. The problems posed force them to confront current issues, such as how to teach diverse students, how schools are funded, and whether or not teaching is recognized as a true profession. We always have numerous issues to draw from. For example, when this particular course (the one I describe in this chapter) was first taught, the Alabama state legislature was embroiled in a debate about whether or not to institute a state lottery to help fund education. I presented this issue as a problem to be explored.

Description of the PBL Assignment

The course was designed around a variety of learning activities. On the first day of the course, I administered to students a learning preferences inventory and discussed the variety of teaching and learning styles that must be accommodated in a classroom. In Classes 2–4, I provided background on the historical roots of education and gave a comprehensive test. In Class 5, I divided the students into groups, making sure each group had members of each learning preference, and gave them an introductory problem, "Investigating PBL." (This problem is available at http://www.samford.edu/schools/education/EDUC320.htm.) They were to explore problem-based learning and the problem-solving process, taking informal notes. To help students with their work, I wrote headings for a PBL chart on the board (see Figure 1.1).

Students read the problem and brainstormed ideas for each column. I walked around the room and sat in on each group. They then conducted research on the Internet. After about 45 minutes, all groups came together, and we filled in the chart on the board. The class next discussed what they had learned about PBL and about problem solving from the process.

For Class 6, each group was given a different problem. I reminded students of the strategy introduced in the previous class

Figure 1.1 HEADINGS FOR A PBL CHART			
What We Know	**Learning Issues**	**What We Need to Know**	**Where to Seek Information**

and asked them to use the same process to begin to explore their problem. I met with each group for 15–30 minutes to monitor their thinking, ask questions, and provide some guidance. Students used the remaining class time to meet in their groups, plan, and determine what each member would research for the next class. I gave each group the name, phone number, and address of the local school administrator who had agreed to be available to advise them. Students were instructed to contact their administrator-mentor and visit that person's school. Information from this visit would be included in their final project.

For Class 7, I once again met for 15–20 minutes with each group to monitor their initial progress in understanding the problem and in locating resources, and to answer process questions. For Classes 8 and 9, all students were required to come to class for roll, then allowed the full class period to work on their problem. They could use the time to research, plan, or visit their mentor. Classes 10 and 11 were devoted to group presentations.

I wrote eight problems for the course. Four are included here as Problems 1–4 (Figures 1.2–1.5 on pp. 12–15). Problems 1 and 2 are examples of problems that different groups explored in Classes 6–11. All groups researched Problems 3 and 4, with each problem culminating in a written piece and an open class discussion.

Classes 12–14 explored the issue of equity funding (see Figure 1.4). The last seven classes of the semester focused on the philosophical basis for education. Learning activities in Classes 15–17 included lectures, followed by a comprehensive test and brief clips from recent movies, such as *Mr. Holland's Opus* and *Dead Poets' Society*, to provoke discussion of educational philosophies. In Class 18, I gave all students Problem 4, along with the full text

---

Figure 1.2
PROBLEM 1: CAN MELANIE MEASURE UP?

Problem Presentation

Melanie, one of your best friends, comes to you. She is graduating from the teacher education program in which you are both enrolled. She is getting married in June, three weeks after she graduates, and will be moving to a town where her spouse is working. She has been to the university placement office to ask if they have any information on the school system in the town and the prospects for a teaching position. The placement director told her that the personnel director would be on campus for Interview Day and gave her a copy of a letter from the district. She was particularly drawn to this paragraph:

> Our school district has many openings. We have several new schools, and our pay scale is as high as any in the region. As with all systems, we are looking for bright, energetic teachers who understand the teaching-learning process. Prospective candidates need to be aware that our students come from diverse socioeconomic backgrounds. We need to be convinced in the interview that they have a serious interest in working with these students and that they want to learn about them and their cultural traditions. The right attitude and hard work are needed to be successful in our district.

Melanie really wants a job in this district. How can you help her? What does she need to know about diversity before her interview? What knowledge and understandings will help her be successful?

Suggestions for a Performance or Product

Your group will decide how you will present your findings. You may use one of the suggestions below or any that your group decides on:

- Class presentation using technology.
- Interview with personnel director.
- Skit followed by discussion.

Learning Issues

How do the following topics affect the issue of diversity?

- Socioeconomic status
- Social class
- Poverty
- Race
- Ethnicity
- Language proficiency

What are some early intervention programs?
What is multicultural education?
Where can a teacher go for help?

---

of the local newspaper articles listing standardized test scores of all local schools and "report card" scores of the schools. A third article detailed the firing of 50 local teachers and administrators because of failure to bring up test scores. In Classes 18–20, the groups explored Problem 4.

Figure 1.3
PROBLEM 2: TEACHER BASHING

Problem Presentation

It was 3:15 p.m. Sarah and John sat down in the teachers' lounge to rest a few minutes before going back to their classrooms to prepare for the next day.

"Did you see the editorial in the morning paper about teachers?" Sarah asked.

"Yeah," sighed John, "more teacher bashing. If the public understood how hard we work, they might have a different appreciation for teachers."

"Why are they always criticizing our profession?" asked Sarah. "You certainly don't read articles criticizing doctors with the same intensity!"

"Well," John responded, "I think the reason may be that people don't consider teaching as a profession in the same way that they view medicine."

Sarah was incensed. "What do you mean teaching is not considered as much a profession as medicine?! What does it mean to be a profession? How can we help people recognize teaching as a profession?"

"I agree that it's a problem," John said. "At the same time, something needs to be done to ensure that only well-qualified teachers are in the classroom. Do standards for teachers need to be raised? Do they need to be more uniform?"

"Maybe if everyone in the United States were teaching the same curriculum, kids from some areas would not seem to be lacking and the teachers would not look so bad," Sarah responded.

"All I know," John said, "is that those of us entering education have got to find a way to bring recognition to the profession of teaching. There must be things we can do."

Suggestions for a Performance or Product

Are Sarah's and John's concerns valid? How can teachers address these concerns? Present to the class your findings about teaching as a profession. You may make your presentation in any way that will inform the class and be interesting. Here are suggestions, but you are not limited to them:

- Class presentation using technology.
- Skit followed by discussion.
- Debate.

Learning Issues

What is a profession?
Is teaching a profession?
How can we ensure the best teachers for *all* children?
Does each school system require the same level of competence from its teachers?
Should teacher certification requirements be standardized?
How can standards for teachers be raised?
Should teachers take a national licensure exam?
Should schools have a national curriculum?

Instructor's Role

To create a successful PBL experience, the instructor must invest considerable time before the first class meeting. I wrote and rewrote problems, attempting to focus on major educational issues.

Figure 1.4
Problem 3: No Lottery! Now What?

Problem Presentation

You and several of your friends are sitting in the university food court drinking a cup of coffee and looking at the morning paper.

David speaks up, "It's hard to realize that it has been a full year since the lottery was defeated. Thank goodness it didn't pass. We sure didn't need all the headaches a lottery would bring!"

"I agree, I guess," Marcy responds. "To be honest, I had a hard time deciding how to vote. The lottery seems to be working in Georgia. And I know it sure would help my family to have free tuition for me and my two younger brothers."

"Well," you put in, "I'm not a big fan of a lottery. But we've got to do something about funds for education. I spent the first half of this semester working in an urban school. Was it ever a lot different from the schools I attended, especially my high school! I kept asking myself, 'Why?' and never got a satisfactory answer. It's bound to be tied to funding—how schools are funded in the state. But why do some schools in the state seem to have so much and others so little?"

"Some of these editorials make me so mad," Meg explodes, "especially these Letters to the Editor! People seem to only look at one side of the issue—no gambling . . . no taxes. What happened to, 'How can we make K–12 schools better?' No one seems to be talking about that! No one seems to care about the simple issue of fairness! Where are all those plans that people promised last year that they would propose and support if the lottery didn't pass?"

"Well," says Anita. "I know that my parents pay a lot more taxes than people in some other areas. Why should their tax money go to schools in other communities?"

"There's got to be a way to be more fair to everyone," Marcy says. "How much *do* people pay in taxes throughout the state? What taxes go toward education? Why does funding seem so unbalanced? How does Alabama compare to other states? What can be done?"

"You're right! And I have an idea," David speaks up. "The newspaper is asking for ideas. Why don't we write our own letter to the editor? Let's give a perspective based on reason rather than just on emotion—try to help people focus on the real issues and what they can do about them."

Suggestion for a Product

As a group, write a letter to the editor proposing a plan to improve funding for education. Give clear reasons for your plan. Be convincing and support your position.

Learning Issues

Where does funding for education come from?

What specific taxes support education funding?

How does tax support for education differ for each state?

What is the evidence that funding for education in [name any state] is adequate or inadequate?

What does the term *equity funding* mean?

What is the evidence that funding for education is equitable or inequitable throughout the state?

How can funding for education be improved for all students?

Figure 1.5
PROBLEM 4: HOW CAN WE IMPROVE TEST SCORES?

Problem Presentation

You are a first-year teacher in grade [your group can decide]. It is Tuesday afternoon, and the faculty is sitting in the library ready for this week's faculty meeting. Suddenly, Mr. Andrews, the principal, enters, a solemn look on his usually cheerful face. He is holding up a copy of an article just published in the local newspaper—the "report card" for all public schools in the metropolitan area—based primarily on the scores of the previous spring's standardized tests.

"I'm certain you have all seen this article showing our school's grade of a *C–*. I have been on the telephone this morning with Dr. Simple, the superintendent of the school district, who is very concerned about our score. It makes us all look bad. I want you to work together on your faculty teams to come up with a plan for how your team will improve test scores next year.

"You realize, of course, that simply saying, 'There is too much emphasis on the tests' is not the answer. There is no way around the importance that the public places on these multiple-choice tests."

[*Note to instructors:* Alabama administers the Stanford Achievement Test. Instructors should focus the problem on the types of standardized tests used in their area.]

Product

Each team will produce a two- to three-page written report that shows how you plan to teach your students to accomplish your team's goals. Each report will include but not be limited to the following:

- Team goals. What do you want to accomplish with your students next year?
- Team philosophy. What do you believe about how children learn?
- Learning theories that serve as the basis for how you will approach the teaching process.
- Types of curricula that are most appropriate.
- Teaching strategies you will use.

The written report is due _____. All teams are to be prepared for an open class discussion on that day.

For months, I perused the local newspaper and national newsmagazines for just the right articles and editorials that might spark an interest or push a button in students. I talked with local school administrators, explaining my goals and enlisting their help as mentors. I set up a management system using a tent card[1] for each student to establish groups and take roll, and I created a Web site

---

[1] A tent card is a rectangular (5″ x 8″) piece of card-stock paper folded in half on which a student's name is written. It stands (like a tent) so that the instructor and other students can easily read the name.

with links (listed at the end of this chapter) so students could begin their search for information. I created assessment documents to measure quality of work and student participation.

While students worked on their problems, I viewed my role as tutor and guide. I met with each group twice at scheduled times and then made myself available to meet with any group to answer questions or clarify assignments. Because one major objection to PBL is that students have trouble finding time to meet with group members, students were given three full class periods to work on their problems. I required students to come to class for roll—sophomore students often need the structure—and then allowed groups to work any place they wished.

One of the most important roles for the instructor is to continually assess the teaching process itself. I observed and listened to my students and asked them to evaluate their learning experiences and the appropriateness of the assignments. I made changes during the first course to address student concerns. For example, originally Problem 3 culminated with group presentations. In response to student feedback that too many presentations were boring, the culminating event became a class discussion. This same assessment stimulated revisions before teaching the course the second time. The revisions are discussed under Problems in this chapter.

Assessment

To culminate the first set of group problems (Problems 1 and 2), each group made a 30-minute presentation, which all class members and I evaluated. The evaluation form is shown in Figure 1.6. To complete Problems 3 and 4, we discussed them in class, and each student had to write a paper, which I evaluated using criteria I had given to the students. Grades on all group presentations and papers accounted for one half of each student's final grade. The other half of the grade was based on individual grades on tests and the course portfolio. The portfolio consisted of students' reflections on each problem and on their growth as learners through the semester.

Figure 1.6
FORM FOR EVALUATING GROUP WORK ON A PRESENTATION

Names of Group Members: _____
Issue: _____

Instructions: Please rate this presentation on the following scale:
1 = Group did not seem well prepared.
2 = Group seemed prepared but not stimulating.
3 = Group seemed well prepared, clear, and stimulating.

Criterion	Rating
Issue was presented clearly.	
Issue was based on facts and data.	
Presenters appeared to be knowledgeable about the issue.	
Presentation provided new and useful information to me.	
Presentation was interesting, informative, and creative.	

Points I learned from this presentation:
1.
2.
3.

Questions I have:
1.
2.
3.

Name of Evaluator: _____ Date: _____

As part of the assessment process, I asked students to evaluate the contributions of each group member as well as their own work. I held conferences with students whose peers indicated that they had not participated appropriately, and I lowered the student's individual grade on the project. I always have students who do not want to grade their peers. I do not dictate what their responses must be and say nothing if they give everyone in the group a perfect score. I believe, however, that I should have the opportunity to hold accountable the group members who do not do their share. I have found that, in every course, most students

Figure 1.7
FORM FOR EVALUATING A MEMBER'S PARTICIPATION IN A GROUP

Name of Group Member Being Evaluated: _____

Instructions: Evaluate your peer using the criteria below. Rate each criterion from 1 to 4, with 4 denoting the best rating. The highest possible score is 20. Be fair and honest.

Criterion	Rating
Attended group meetings and was on time.	
Contributed to the overall group plan.	
Accepted a fair share of responsibility for the project.	
Completed assigned tasks on time.	
Helped others when appropriate.	
Total	

What percentage of the work did this person complete?

What was this person's most significant contribution?

Other Comments:

want the opportunity to evaluate their team members and themselves. Figure 1.7 is a form to evaluate the work of a group member; Figure 1.8 is a self-evaluation form.

The first time I taught the course as PBL, I created forms to assess students' problem-solving abilities, process skills, and attitudes. I quickly learned that unless one adult tutor can consistently be with every group of no more than seven members, such assessments are not possible. They are best pursued in settings with small groups and tutors.

Outcomes

I believe that confronting current issues, becoming aware of attitudes about education in the popular press, and working as teams to thoroughly research issues and generate solutions had a positive effect on the students. The high quality of their presentations as well as comments from their reflective journals reinforced

---

Figure 1.8
FORM FOR A SELF-EVALUATION

Your Name: _____

Instructions: Evaluate your work in the group using the criteria below. Rate each criterion from 1 to 4, with 4 denoting the best rating. The highest possible score is 20. Be fair and honest.

Criterion	Rating
Attended group meetings and was on time.	
Contributed to the overall group plan.	
Accepted a fair share of responsibility for the project.	
Completed assigned tasks on time.	
Helped others when appropriate.	
Total	

What percentage of the work did you complete?

What was your most significant contribution?

Other Comments:

---

this perception. I found that students benefitted in the following ways; their journal comments reflect the same idea:

• Took ownership of issues and recognized the effect on their professional lives.

Journal comments: "I am now ready to fight this [negative] public image. I realized that changing this starts with me. I am ready to involve myself with the professional organizations and get ideas going. I learned the importance of putting 110 percent into my first year of teaching."

• Connected the issues and understood the relationship of the course to their lives.

Journal comments: "I liked the class because of the interesting subject matter we were presented with. I felt a connection with the material and realized that it was not just a grade, but that it was affecting me as a person. I cannot say that about many of the classes I have taken until now. This made me feel excited because it confirmed that teaching was my passion."

• Learned the value of working as a team and of using perseverance to solve a problem.

Journal comments: "It was definitely beneficial to have all five of us working on the same problem to come to some solid conclusion. Had I been working on this project by myself, my outcome would have been quite different."

Journal comments: "The first thing I honestly learned was to not give up when faced with a tough problem. We thought for a fact that we would have no substantial arguments the day of the debate. But through persistence we pulled ourselves through and firmly held our stance for vouchers."

• Began to appreciate the historical and philosophical contexts of current educational practice.

Journal comments: "When did John Dewey live? You mean that PBL is not a new educational fad?"

Problems

One major problem was the large class size. All PBL workshops I had attended and the programs I had visited recommended groups of no more than seven, with a trained tutor for every group. Many experts argue that true PBL exists only in such a situation. My question was, Could I make PBL work in my classes of 45 and 56 students, with one instructor?

I found that I had to make concessions, some of which I mentioned earlier:

• I had to create a way to manage groups and avoid chaos. Tent cards, which I made after the first class, were a big help. I put the cards on tables to designate an assigned group so that students could easily find their group. To take roll, I merely removed the cards of missing students from the tables.

• I had to give up some original assessment expectations. I could not observe every student and assess individual problem-solving abilities. I believe that this inability to make such assessments is a major disadvantage of using groups in a large class.

• I had to find a way to meet with each group to help them get started. I originally wanted to give the groups complete autonomy. But I realized that these were sophomores who needed some guidance and reassurance from the teacher and who, generally, would not ask. For these reasons, I scheduled two meetings with each group as they began their first problem and checked in with each group on succeeding class days.

• With nine or more groups, having every group work and report on every problem was redundant and boring. No one felt truly responsible for the knowledge. To alleviate this concern, I assigned different problems to each group and required them to teach their peers about their issue.

• I solicited school administrators to serve as resources for the groups. Visiting the schools helped students see the relevance of the issues.

I continue to grapple with some concerns. For example, if every group has a different issue, how can I be certain everyone in the class gets the most important information? I now require each group to prepare a one- to two-page handout for all class members. Each group lists succinctly, in bullet format, the main points. During class discussion, I add any major concepts they may have missed. The final exam comes from these lists.

Students tell me they would like more direction as they begin researching their issues—to help them narrow the scope of their investigations. I understand their frustrations with limited time. I want to give them as much freedom as possible, however, to search, analyze, and think for themselves. I continue to work with students to find the right balance, and I created Web pages with links to helpful resources (see Additional Resources at the end of this chapter).

Suggestions and Conclusions

I believe that teacher education majors need to understand how PBL can be used as a strategy for teaching and learning; how it enhances their own learning; and how to use PBL in their own classrooms. With these goals in mind, I began the first class of the course by administering a learning preferences inventory and explained what the inventory meant for them as learners and as teachers with diverse learners in their classrooms. We talked about PBL as a strategy that is particularly comfortable for certain types of learners and uncomfortable for others. We talked about teaching so that each learner is often comfortable and stretched.

On the second class day, we talked about PBL as a learning strategy. We frankly discussed student successes and frustrations in their experiences with PBL before this course. Students were to reflect on this discussion in their portfolios and determine whether they felt they had a clearer understanding of PBL at the end of the course.

Throughout their education program at Samford, students expand their understanding of PBL. The teacher education curriculum has been carefully designed so students will have a variety of experiences with PBL as they move through their coursework. In their senior year, they learn to design and teach a PBL unit for their classes.

Faculty members agree that telling future teachers there is only one way to teach would be a disservice. To meet the needs of diverse learners, teachers must use a variety of strategies and maintain a balance in their classrooms. In this course and in the subsequent curriculum, students encounter traditional lectures and tests as well as active learning strategies other than PBL.

I am convinced that PBL is an excellent way to engage students in material that might otherwise seem irrelevant. Confronting them with real issues, providing mentors who are practicing educators to help them gain a broader perspective, and giving them the responsibility to teach their classmates are powerful ways to help students begin to explore and take ownership of their future profession.

ADDITIONAL RESOURCES

Dean, C. (1998). *Education 320: Foundations of education* [Online course description]. Birmingham, AL: Samford University. Available: http://www.samford.edu/schools/education/EDUC320.htm (2000, November 27).

A Web site giving students access to problems used in the course. It provides links to sources of information that will help in researching educational issues.

Samford University School of Education. (2000). *Center for problem-based learning research and communications* [Web site]. Birmingham, AL: Samford University. Available: http://www.samford.edu/pbl (2000, September 21).

A Web site created by the Problem-Based Learning Center at Samford University. It provides information on where and how PBL is applied in undergraduate institutions throughout the world. It also provides an extensive bibliography for PBL.

Samford University School of Education. (n.d.). *Problem-based learning* [Web site]. Birmingham, AL: Samford University. Available: http://www.samford.edu/schools/education/pbl/pbl_index.html (2000, September 21).

A Web site providing background information from the literature about PBL. It explains why PBL strategies are important for teaching and learning in teacher education and in K–12. It also links to a unit plan outline and a sample PBL unit developed at Samford University and to sites that provide answers to questions about PBL and offer sample problems.

Problem-Based Learning in an Undergraduate Educational Psychology Course

LEE SHUMOW

I DESIGNED FOUR PROBLEM-BASED LEARNING (PBL) UNITS FOR AN INTRO-
ductory undergraduate course entitled Educational Psychology. The
course is required for students seeking elementary school teacher
certification and introduces the research on learning to prospective
elementary school teachers. Its goal is to help students apply educational psychology research to teaching early in their professional
preparation sequence. The PBL units I discuss in this chapter address the concern that student teachers do not transfer knowledge
from their coursework on learning to their practice in the field.

Context for PBL

Two sections of students, who had enrolled in a one-semester
(14 weeks) Educational Psychology course, participated in four
PBL units. Each unit corresponded to one fourth of the course content. During the first half of the semester (first seven weeks), Section 1 students worked on Problems 1 and 2, while Section 2 students studied the corresponding content in a traditional college
class format. The traditional format entailed studying the material
one concept at a time. I made presentations, showed examples of
concepts, and involved students in discussions by posing questions

about the content. During the second half of the semester (second seven weeks), Section 2 worked on Problems 3 and 4, while Section 1 (initial PBL group) studied the same material in a traditional college class format. Students worked individually and in assigned groups to solve each problem over a three-week period.

On the first class day of the PBL half of the semester, I gave students handouts containing an overview of PBL, guidelines for working on the problems, requirements, and grading expectations. Small groups of four to five students were formed for each problem so that individuals could gain experience working with a variety of other students. I assigned groups by asking students to draw a number corresponding to a group number (one to six). Three groups worked on Problem 1 (or Problem 3), while three worked on Problem 2 (or Problem 4). After spending three weeks on a problem, groups shared and discussed their solutions with the entire class. They then switched problems and followed the same process.

Each small group met with me once a week for 30 minutes. During the remaining class time, students planned what they would do. They could conduct individual research or meet together to solve the problem. In any course, a typical complaint of students who are assigned group projects is that they cannot meet outside of class because of conflicting schedules. To address this concern, students could use regularly scheduled class time for meetings.

Purposes for Using PBL

The goals for the PBL units were to help students gain content knowledge, strengthen problem-solving skills, engage in learning, and develop a professional identity. A related goal, consistent with the recent call for reform in teaching educational psychology (Anderson, Blumenfeld, Pintrich, Clark, Marx, & Peterson, 1995), was to make classroom practices for teaching prospective teachers consonant with research knowledge about best practices that promote student learning and engagement—such as PBL.

Figure 2.1
PROBLEM 1: CHAOS IN THE 5TH GRADE

You are a 5th grade teacher in an elementary school. The entire 5th grade class has be-havior problems. Numerous playground fights have occurred, and two have been serious enough to send children to the hospital, one with a broken finger and the other with a concussion. The children don't get along in class either. Bickering and fighting have dis-rupted class routines, and students are not accomplishing small-group tasks, which are the centerpiece of the language arts curriculum. They seem more interested in dis-cussing prime-time television shows than the literature they are reading. For the upcoming unit on folk and fairy tales, the teacher's guide for the literature-based reading books says, "Traditional tales offer opportunities for the promotion of conflict resolution skills." The guide offers no further explanation.

The first round of parent conferences has just ended, and many parents asked about the behavior problem issue. You heard about quieter children not wanting to come to school and about children—who had acted aggressively at school—complaining to their parents that they were picked on and treated unfairly by peers and school staff. Parents also complained about recess being taken away from all children for the misbehavior of "the group."

The 5th grade teachers have called for a meeting to deal with this crisis. How will you and the other teachers get this problem under control and help children develop the self-control needed for the remainder of the school year and expected in middle school?

Description of the PBL Assignment

We devoted three weeks of class and study time to working on each of the four PBL problems. The issues in Problem 1 (Figure 2.1) deal with concepts of social competence, temperament differ-ences, self-regulation, and behavioral problems among 5th graders on the playground and in the classroom. This problem addresses the topics of personal, social, and emotional development; man-aging the learning environment; social cognitive theory; and work-ing with parents.

Problem 2 (Figure 2.2) centers on mathematics learning in the primary grades. Topics addressed include human memory, con-ceptual learning, instructional strategies, and assessment.

Problem 3 (Figure 2.3 on p. 28) deals with learning goals in 4th grade social studies and science. The topics addressed are higher-order thinking skills (critical thinking and problem solving), instructional strategies, assessment, and parental involvement.

Figure 2.2
PROBLEM 2: "FORGOTTEN" MATH FACTS IN THE 2ND GRADE

You are the 1st grade teachers in a district serving predominately white, middle-income children in a white-collar county of the Chicago metropolitan area. Based on demographic information, your district does not qualify for funds directed toward improving the educational opportunities for impoverished or underrepresented populations.

The 2nd grade teachers have complained to the curriculum coordinator that students are arriving in 2nd grade with minimal knowledge of the basic math facts. You use the same mathematics program that the district has used for 10 years. An examination of the curriculum shows that children have plenty of practice with drill on basic math facts. What could explain the children's memory loss, and what are you going to do about it?

To compound matters, a community member has made a presentation to the school board decrying the educational trend away from memorization of facts in the school curriculum. He argued that more time needs to be devoted to rote drill of facts so that achievement will increase. The local newspaper featured an article on his views. Recent scores on the Iowa Tests of Basic Skills indicate that elementary students in the district are functioning slightly above the state average on mathematics computation, but average student performance on mathematical concepts is below the national average. Students scored considerably above average on total reading, reading comprehension, and social studies on the Iowa tests.

The principal is expected to present a response to the citizen complaint at the next board meeting. As dedicated teachers, you are quite concerned about the mathematics learning of your students. Using information on memory and research on learning (especially on mathematics learning), formulate a plan to address this problem in your classrooms. Prepare information that will guide you in implementing it and that can be shared with the principal, 2nd grade teachers, school board members, parents, and other citizens.

Problem 4 (Figure 2.4 on p. 29) focuses on a situation in an elementary school. A disproportionate number of minority students performed considerably below average academically on the state achievement test. Topics from the course include cultural and language differences in learning, instructional grouping, inequitable educational practices, and culturally responsive teaching.

Guidelines for Working on the Problems

We discussed the course expectations and guidelines as a large group. I told students I expected them to work independently and in teams to solve the problem posed by the situation. One guideline explicitly stated that students should first try to understand

---

Figure 2.3
PROBLEM 3: DEMAND FOR HIGHER-ORDER LEARNING IN THE 4TH GRADE

The Illinois State Board of Education has established learning goals for students. The curriculum and instruction coordinator for the school district that employs you as a 4th grade teacher notes that your district has been doing a good job at addressing some of the goals *except* those that entail promoting higher-level thinking skills for students in social studies and science. The district administration has decided that asking each grade-level team to design a plan and incorporating the learning goals into classroom instruction will address this problem. The superintendent has asked that parents and interested others in the community be well informed about the changes, because some communities have opposed school reform. Based on literature the superintendent has read, she has decided that much of this opposition results from misinformation and insufficient understanding.

You are on a team of 4th grade teachers charged with integrating these learning goals into the district curriculum for 4th grade. Such work entails designing a district teachers' guide in which you identify components of higher-order thinking skills; show how they can be fostered in 4th grade social studies and science; explain why such skills are important; and provide an example of how higher-order thinking will be promoted within the current social studies and science unit topics. For this example, specify what students will be expected to learn during the unit (aligned with state goals and higher-order thinking skills) and how students will learn it (e.g., through curriculum content and instructional principles); identify how you will know if students used these skills; and provide a plan for keeping parents informed about the goals, process, content, and assessments presented in the unit.

---

the nature of the problem by asking themselves several questions, including, What is wrong here? What are the factors involved? What kind of problem is this? What do I know about this problem? What do I need to know? Where can I find out more?

Another guideline asked them to generate possible solutions to the issues, using their understanding of the problem and the research they had conducted as a basis. A related guideline asked students to explain why their proposed solutions would address the particular problem. To reassure those students who were oriented to getting the "right" answer, I recommended the following strategy in the guidelines and repeated the idea often when meeting with students:

> As in many real situations, the problems presented are fuzzy, and there is no one right answer. This does not mean that solutions to the situations are merely matters of opinion. You will need to

Figure 2.4
PROBLEM 4: ADDRESSING INEQUITIES IN GROUPING PRACTICES AT AN ELEMENTARY SCHOOL

The school (grades 4–6) in which you teach has a 43 percent minority population (40 percent black, 3 percent other minority). Most (78 percent) of these minority students come from low-income families, whereas only 6 percent of the white children in the district come from low-income families. A majority (85 percent) of minority students are performing considerably below average academically, and the minority student suspension rate is five times the majority student suspension rate.

A minority advocacy group has threatened to sue the school district. It claims that tracking (academic ability grouping) is a form of segregation and that the low achievement scores are indicators of discrimination. A coalition representing community churches has expressed concern and called upon its membership to support the school in its attempt to address inequities and raise achievement of minority children. The school board has promised the community that they will solve this problem fairly. They plan to showcase the efforts of a team of exemplary teachers who are succeeding with all children.

You are on the assigned language arts team. You were selected because the principal recognized your talent and commitment to improving learning among all students. How have you accomplished your success? Present guidelines for raising the achievement of all children, using equitable and effective grouping practices.

reason about these situations using evidence from what is currently known from research or principled practice about these topics. Some solutions *are* better than others because there are reasons to believe that certain solutions will be more effective than others. The key is to generate ideas, support them, and consider their limitations. It is through reasoning with knowledge that you can determine which solutions are likely to be most effective.

Requirements

To aid communication with each other and with me, I told students I expected them to use their student e-mail accounts. A required textbook (Eggen & Kauchak, 1999) served as a starting point for student reading and research on the problems. To avoid scheduling conflicts, I encouraged students to meet with their groups during regularly scheduled class time.

Each student was required to keep a log that showed individual work. A spiral notebook or a looseleaf binder worked well. Log entries were grouped into four categories, shown in Figure 2.5 (see p. 30).

Figure 2.5
KEEPING A STUDENT LOG

Instructions: Use a log to keep track of the research you conduct. Entries in the log should contain the following headings:

List of sources, such as completed readings, Web sites visited, media viewed, and experts interviewed. Be specific in source citations. Include enough information so that another person could locate the material. Textbook chapters and pages are provided on the course syllabus as *starting points* for your investigation. Textbook information is insufficient, so you will need to research beyond it. Use extensively the Web address list you will be given. Check the handout that lists articles reserved for you in the library. Many have useful information.

Written responses to what you read, saw, or heard. Discuss what you learned from each reading, Web site, media, or expert interview. Include both what was helpful and not helpful in thinking about the problem you are trying to solve. *Be a critical thinker.*

Suggestions for solving the problem and your reasons for why the suggestions would be beneficial (using the research you did). Contribute these to your group during meetings.

Brief descriptions of what was discussed in small-group meetings. What were the suggestions? What decisions were made and why? Reflect on these decisions. Were they good ones? Why or why not? What reservations do you have?

Grading Expectations

In an attempt to avoid "free riders," I asked each student to affirm on a checklist whether each of the other group members had contributed sufficiently to the group. If more than one group member identified another member as not contributing, I examined the student's attendance pattern, e-mail communications with me and their group members (which were copied to me), and log for evidence of whether the student had shirked responsibility. The penalty for not contributing was a drop in one letter grade. I investigated three complaints; two students received a grade reduction after meeting with me to discuss their work.

Instructor's Role

I designed the four PBL units during one summer, using procedures on how to develop effective PBL units described by the Illinois Math and Science Academy's (1998) Center for Problem-Based Learning (CPBL). First, I drew on problem situations from my experience as a teacher, supervisor, researcher, and teacher educator in public elementary schools. Planning required balancing the course content and problem situations. I created a situation map describing the specific details of the problem situation and developed a list of concepts that could be abstracted from the problem. (For an example of a situation map, see the CPBL Web site [IMSA, 1998] listed in References.) The course outline, the situation map, and the concept list determined which subject matter from the course matched each problem. Finally, I adapted problems and roles to fit the course outline and prepared the handouts explained earlier.

I met with each group at least three times—once a week for three weeks. During these meetings, students summarized their progress, contributed individual ideas, and planned what to do next. Initially, my role was to make sure that they had defined the problem thoroughly and to refocus them on the goal or on elements of the problem that they had overlooked. I also suggested resources. As students began to work on the problem and consider solutions, I asked them to justify their ideas with concepts or knowledge from their research and reading. If students were stuck, I would ask them leading questions to guide them or provide them with essential pieces of information and then ask them to apply the information to the problem. Students could also ask me questions by e-mail, during office hours, or before and after class. They frequently contacted me before or after class; their visits during office hours and e-mail contacts were similar to those in the more traditional courses I have taught.

Assessment

I assessed student work for the semester in two areas: content knowledge and problem solving. I asked the students to assess PBL.

Content Knowledge

All students took four objective tests on content knowledge for the course. Each test included 10 multiple-choice questions, which asked them to identify definitions or examples of concepts from the topics covered. For example, Test 1 dealt with limit setting, promoting self-regulated work habits, conflict resolution, fostering social competence, logical consequences, and moral development. Test 2 focused on memory, conceptual learning, and communication with parents. Test 3 emphasized problem solving, critical thinking, self-regulated learning, and learner-centered principles. Test 4 covered ability grouping, cultural influences on learning, cooperative grouping, and effective practices for at-risk students.

Problem Solving

Students wrote an essay describing how they solved a problem that was parallel to the problem they had worked on. These problem solution essays were evaluated on four dimensions drawn from the problem-solving literature: defining the problem (conceptual issues, goals, and type of problems); generating solutions; justifying solutions; and organizing the essay. A fifth dimension evaluated mechanical errors (e.g., spelling, grammar, and punctuation). I developed a four-point scale to evaluate each dimension, shown in Figure 2.6. The presentations or logs could be evaluated using the same or a similar rubric.

Student Evaluation of PBL

On the final day of the semester, all students completed a questionnaire. Several items asked them to compare the PBL portion of the class to the traditional portion in terms of their motivation, learning of content, application of content, and professional development, indicating whether PBL was better, equal to, or worse than the traditional class. Other items asked students to rate the educational value of various aspects of the PBL experience, such as group work, individual research, and keeping a log. Additional open-ended items allowed students to elaborate on their ideas about PBL.

Figure 2.6
RUBRIC FOR ESSAYS ON PROBLEM SOLUTION

Level of Work	DIMENSION				
	Defining the Problem	Generating Solutions	Justifying Solutions	Organizing the Essay	Evaluating the Mechanics of the Essay
1	Identified no concepts or identified concepts that were unclear and not applicable.	Did not generate adequate solutions.	Provided no evidence to support solutions.	Wrote an unclear and disorganized essay.	Made numerous errors in grammar, spelling, and punctuation.
2	Identified concepts that were vague or had some inaccuracies or both.	Generated one adequate solution.	Provided weak or incomplete justification to support solutions.	Wrote an essay with some disorganized and unclear sections.	Made four to eight errors in grammar, spelling, and punctuation.
3	Identified most concepts.	Generated two adequate solutions.	Provided some rational justification to support solutions.	Wrote a reasonably organized and clear essay.	Made less than four errors in grammar, spelling, and punctuation.
4	Identified all concepts thoroughly.	Generated multiple solutions that were clearly related to problem identification.	Provided thorough justification with evidence to support solutions.	Wrote a well-organized and clear essay.	Made no errors in grammar, spelling, and punctuation.

Outcomes

Some evidence shows that PBL was effective for preparing future teachers to apply the content from educational psychology to problematic situations. Students' grades on objective and essay tests indicate that students in one section learned at least as well from PBL as they did from a traditional format; students in the other section learned better from PBL than they did from the traditional format. Students in both sections reported that they learned more, were more motivated, and had to take more responsibility for their learning during PBL than during traditional instruction. Their written responses to an open-ended probe substantiate these ratings. They said that, for the PBL section, they liked coming to class for PBL more, thought about the problem more, and "felt more like a part of something."

Students believed that the individualized research they conducted was the most educational aspect of PBL. They identified PBL as valuable for learning content knowledge, developing as professionals, and learning how to apply course content to teaching.

Problems

Students who learned through PBL during the first half of the semester performed equally, but not better, on assessments compared to the traditionally taught students in the other section. One possible reason that students in the first section did not perform better might be that I was using PBL for the first time in this course. Anecdotal evidence suggests that the students using PBL during the first half of the semester were reluctant to discuss their thinking about the problem with me during the meeting times. Rather, they expressed concern about having the right answer. Students who had more exposure to my viewpoint on the importance of seeking multiple solutions, which I expressed in class discussions during the traditional instructional period, were probably more comfortable with the idea of generating and evaluating possible solutions.

In response to an open-ended evaluation item, students noted frustration with free riders in the collaborative groups (Salamon & Globerson, 1989), although small-group collaboration was rated highly for promoting learning. Thus, students' generally positive attitude toward the educational value of group work was tempered by a problem that arose with several individuals who did not contribute sufficiently to their groups. This problem occurred despite holding students individually accountable for their learning and work.

Another issue involved students who did not seem attuned to the educational value of listening to what other groups had to say during sharing day. Students seemed unaware that they could use other groups or their logs as resources. Few took notes on other groups' solutions or included in their essays the new ideas or justifications they heard about. They rarely used their logs in writing essays, although the assessment was open book and open note. Students need to be told explicitly about using notes and logs as resources.

Finally, students were quite anxious about the in-class essay examinations. Although they could have improved their essay responses by using the rubric (Figure 2.6) as a guide, few did so. It appears that they needed more direct guidance.

Suggestions and Conclusions

Integrating PBL throughout the entire semester, rather than for half a semester, might have been better for all students. One way is to have students work on problems as individual homework assignments. A second possibility is to use the four problems as an organizing framework for each one fourth of the course. Instructor presentations, media shown in class, and class discussions could then be anchored in the problem. Each class quarter could culminate with students integrating the content in a problem solution essay written either in class or as a take-home assignment. All students would work on four problems, and some traditional instruction would be anchored in each problem. A third possibility is to alternate PBL with traditional methods. For example, problems could be integrated in the second and fourth quarters of the course. A fourth possibility is to use a modified jigsaw approach: Each small group works on a different problem, the groups present their solutions in class, and the student audience assesses the groups' work.

A possible solution to the problem of free riders is to collect logs and check them in each class period to ensure that all students are working toward the solution and routinely contributing to the group. The issue is troublesome because PBL is a simulation during a professional preparation program. As an instructor, I was deeply concerned that free riding suggested that these students might be unreliable future teachers and colleagues, and I questioned if the students should be penalized. On the other hand, I knew that students were individually accountable on their tests and wondered if they should be allowed to pursue learning the material in the way that suited them best or to learn from the consequences of not being prepared for the assessment. More monitoring of group participation may improve implementation.

In conclusion, these PBL units provided some advantages to the students. Students learned at least as much content knowledge as they did in a traditional class. Students in the traditional section at the beginning of the semester improved in problem-solving skills after participating in PBL. Most important, students believed that the PBL units were engaging and relevant to their professional development. Most rated PBL as more engaging than traditional instruction. Although several problems were encountered with using these units, these problems can be addressed in future implementations.

REFERENCES

Anderson, L., Blumenfeld, P., Pintrich, P., Clark, C., Marx, R., & Peterson, P. (1995). Educational psychology for teachers: Reforming our courses, re-thinking our roles. *Educational Psychologist, 30*(3), 143–157.

An article providing reasons and guidelines for reforming educational psychology classes for teachers.

Eggen, P., & Kauchak, D. (1999). *Educational psychology: Windows on classrooms* (4th ed.). Upper Saddle River, NJ: Merrill.

A textbook used in the author's undergraduate educational psychology classes.

Illinois Mathematics and Science Academy (IMSA). (1998). *Center for problem-based learning* [Online]. Available: http://www.imsa.edu/team/cpbl/cpbl.html (2000, November 28).

A Web site containing a wealth of information about developing, planning, and implementing problem-based learning.

Salamon, G., & Globerson, T. (1989). When teams do not function the way they are supposed to. *International Journal of Educational Research, 13*(1), 89–98.

A report about problems with small-group work.

ADDITIONAL RESOURCES

National Commission on Teaching and America's Future. (1996). *What matters most: Teaching for America's future.* New York: National Commission on Teaching and America's Future.

A document describing the importance of preparing teachers who understand student learning and development, and connections with practice.

Shumow, L. (in press). Problem-based learning: Potential contributor to learning and motivation of preservice teachers. *The Professional Educator.*

An article about the classes discussed in this chapter. The article focuses on why differences in learning between the PBL and traditional classes were expected, reports on how learning and motivation were measured, and discusses statistical and qualitative findings.

3 Providing Structure for Analyzing Authentic Problems

Jean W. Pierce and Herbert G. Lange

IN THIS CHAPTER, WE DESCRIBE AN APPROACH TO PROBLEM-BASED LEARN-ing (PBL) that is more structured than some other implementations. Our approach addresses several specific issues faced by educational psychology instructors who want to incorporate PBL into their courses. First, some instructors are concerned about the additional time required for PBL and uncertain about whether students who plot their own course for solving problems acquire basic knowledge. Second, an educational psychology course must incorporate a large body of prescribed information and skills for students to pass certification examinations. Third, educational psychology is typically required early in a student's program, and students who are experiencing PBL for the first time need scaffolding as they develop problem-solving strategies. To help instructors deal with these issues, our approach requires students to complete a series of graphic organizers and other assignments to coach them through the problem-solving process.

Context for PBL

The undergraduate educational psychology course at Northern Illinois University has two primary objectives: Teacher education students must learn to compare and contrast theories of learning and motivation; they must learn to recognize implications from the theories.

Students taking the one-semester (16-week) course are typically college sophomores; a majority are elementary education majors. All have passed introductory psychology; some have completed a course in child development and are anxious to have authentic experiences with children. PBL offers these prospective teachers a means to contextualize learning theories while helping them master a large body of information in a three-credit course (Pierce & Jones, 1999).

During the first half of the semester, we expose students to various theories of learning and motivation. They experience behavioral direct instruction, social learning modeling, and radical and social constructivism, among other theory-driven instructional models. The students plot key principles for each theory on two matrices—one compares and contrasts learning principles, and one focuses on various interpretations of motivation.

During the second half of the semester, they engage in two PBL experiences while they receive instruction and participate in discussions on such topics as objectives, strategies for learning, motivation, assessment, and class management. They show mastery of objectives by satisfactorily completing several assignments for each problem. Students work in groups, but they are graded individually for bringing their own ideas to the group discussions, and they must create their own syntheses of the group's decisions.

Purposes for Using PBL

One major reason for using PBL methods is that they are congruent with the learner-centered psychological principles identified by a task force of the American Psychological Association (1997). These principles are firmly rooted in a wide body of research conducted over a number of years (Alexander & Murphy,

1998). The principles are organized into four categories: cognitive and metacognitive factors, motivation and affect, development and social principles, and individual differences. The approach to PBL we describe addresses these learner-centered principles by

- Showing students how to use matrices for representing the knowledge that they construct.
- Allowing students time to reflect on the teaching-learning process.
- Providing for learner choice and control in a collaborative context.
- Honoring individual perspectives by requiring that students come to class with their own plans.

The course is also congruent with program standards of the Association for Childhood Education International (2000), which makes these recommendations:

- Study and apply current research findings about individual differences and teaching and learning.
- Systematically observe and practice activities that stimulate reflective and critical thinking, problem solving, and decision-making skills.
- Provide systematic feedback and coaching to increase using strategies effectively to promote learning.
- Provide opportunities for practice in matching content, objectives, and teaching behaviors to the selection and analysis of teaching materials for students.

Description of the PBL Assignment

Students complete two PBL problems during the 16-week course. We present Problem 1 (Figure 3.1) during Week 6 and Problem 2 during Week 8.

Figure 3.1
PROBLEM 1: ANALYZING INDIVIDUAL DIFFERENCES IN A CLASS

You will see a videotape showing a class of 25 children in a public elementary school. Your task is to identify individual differences that seem to be present in the classroom—such as diverse cultures, giftedness, learning disabilities, and behavior disorders. What needs and strengths will you encounter when you teach the class? How will you address those needs and strengths in the lesson you present to the class?

Problem 1: Analyzing Individual Differences in a Class

Problem 1 is centered around a videotaped day in a public elementary school classroom and introduces PBL activities that undergraduates will engage in during the remainder of the course.

We create the videotape to provide the same experience for all students in the course. Many enter teacher preparation with definite ideas about what they consider to be good teaching, and their classroom observations are often filtered through these relatively fixed ideas. They only realize this tendency when others who have observed the same classroom situation challenge their perceptions and definitions of the problems.

Resources for Problem 1

The most important resource is a teacher who is confident enough to let her class be videotaped in the third week of the semester. This taping can be difficult during the fall because students and teachers are just getting to know one another and the classroom routines. The teacher must also be willing to answer many questions from the prospective teachers and collaborate with our educational psychology classes. E-mail seems to be the most efficient way to communicate.

The videotaping equipment needs to be good enough for the viewers to understand clearly what the teacher and students say; that is, the teacher needs to be wired for sound. Optimally, two cameras are used—one to record the whole classroom and one to focus on individuals who are speaking. If only one camera is used, one person operates the camera, while the other identifies significant behaviors to direct the cameraperson to. The audio quality does not have to capture every pin drop, but if the sound is weak, we make a transcript of the videotape. The goal is to present enough information for our students to observe the classroom situation. To help identify classroom students, we give undergraduates a class seating chart and pictures of the children.

Requirements for Problem 1

To address Problem 1, we coach students through the following general procedures, which require about six hours of class time:

1. Before class, the undergraduates read two textbook chapters about individual differences among students.

2. The class views the videotape of the elementary school class.

3. Each student records observations that could be evidence for individual differences.

4. Each student identifies three individual differences that seem most salient.

5. Each student completes a matrix (Figure 3.2) to help identify problems. The matrix headings include questions to guide students' analyses; examples in each column provide guideposts toward a possible response.

6. We divide the class into groups of three to five students who share common interests in a particular need or strength in the observed class.

7. The groups work to further define the problem; they may borrow the videotape if needed.

8. Group members each share questions from their matrices (Figure 3.2). The group determines which questions to pursue and where to look for answers.

9. Questions relating to the specific classroom and students are sent by e-mail to the teacher to answer.

Figure 3.2

MATRIX FOR IDENTIFYING INDIVIDUAL DIFFERENCES IN A CLASS

Individual Difference	Specific observation about individual difference. *Rate the certainty of each observation from 1 (very certain) to 4 (very uncertain).*	What strength or need may be present in the class? What does it mean if a class has one or more students with that individual difference?	How is the teacher currently addressing that strength or need?	Questions to ask. *Put the questions in order of priority from most to least important.*	Where will the answer be found—from the teacher or library research?
(Example) Attention deficit	(Example) Students are often out of their seats = 1.	(Example) Students are not paying attention to directions. Work cannot be completed accurately.	(Example) Students earn points for following directions.	(Example) 1. Are they usually out of their seats so much, or were they reacting to the camera? 2. What are the characteristics of attention deficit disorder (ADD)?	(Example) Teacher

Source: Adapted from Pierce & Jones, 1999.

10. Group members obtain and read research articles from the library or the Web to find answers to general questions that they consider most important.

11. Groups hypothesize how various theories of learning and motivation may define and address the needs and strengths of particular students in the videotaped class.

12. Each student completes another matrix to pull together various ways to define and meet those needs and strengths. Figure 3.3 shows an example of how this matrix may be completed for an individual with attention deficit disorder (ADD).

13. Groups choose one way of defining the problem, then develop lists of suggestions for teachers working with that type of individual difference. For example, to add more structure for ADD students, a group might suggest a behavioral solution— charting and reinforcing students' paying attention (see Column 3, Figure 3.3).

14. Students reorganize into groups consisting of one member from each individual-difference work group. These new groups make recommendations for how teachers could deal with a class containing all the needs and strengths identified. For example, these groups might discover that one member is advocating stimulating, self-initiated experiences for a gifted student, while another person is arguing for structure for an ADD student.

15. The class meets with the teacher, who leads a discussion about the feasibility of their suggestions.

Problem 2: Developing a Lesson Plan

Problem 2 (Figure 3.4 on p. 46) builds on the information gathered in Problem 1. The students' task is to develop a lesson plan, which they will present to their class. They have the option of presenting it to the elementary school class.

One week before the class session when the videotaped teacher responds to the undergraduates' suggestions for addressing needs and strengths, she provides general topics that her students will be studying at the end of the semester—for example, fractions, Earth Day, or the states. Course students then select from

Figure 3.3
Sample Matrix for Addressing One Type of Need or Strength

Way to Define a Need or Strength	Suggestions from That Perspective	General Suggestions	Suggestions When Teaching a Lesson
Teacher's most useful answer: (Example) One child has been diagnosed with ADD.	This is a valid concern for the class.	Help students develop their abilities to determine what they should pay attention to. Monitor whether they are or have been paying attention.	Assign one person to look at specific children to make sure they are paying attention.
Behaviorism: Students may be reinforced for not paying attention.	Consider whether the teacher interacts more with students who have not been paying attention.	Chart and reinforce students' paying attention.	
Social learning: Students may not pay attention if they do not feel they can learn.	Consider the self-efficacy of the students.	Show students that they are learning.	
Information processing: Students may have too many things commanding their attention.	Help students focus on the important information.	Help students monitor whether they have been paying attention.	
Constructivism: From the teacher's perspective, students may not be able to figure out why they should pay attention.	Invite students to think about their role in paying attention.	Ask students why they should pay attention.	
Most useful ideas from research: Students with ADD may have poor handwriting and organizational skills.	Make sure students clearly understand the information.	Present information using graphic organizers.	

Figure 3.4
Problem 2: Developing a Lesson Plan

How would your group plan, deliver, and evaluate a lesson for students like those
in the videotape? Consider the following topics in your work: purposes for learning,
information processing, thinking skills, motivation, assessment, transfer, and classroom
management.

---

these topics those that interest them the most. They form groups
around these topics. Each group of four to five students is charged
with the task of developing one lesson, which they will present to
the elementary class.

On the day when the teacher meets with our students to respond to their recommendations for accommodating individual
differences (Problem 1), she also meets with the lesson-planning
groups (Problem 2). The undergraduates have already begun to
develop questions that they need to have answered before they can
present their lessons to their classmates. During the meeting, the
teacher often gives them her telephone number and e-mail address, encouraging them to contact her with other questions.

For the next six weeks, whenever a topic (e.g., objectives, class
management, or assessment) is assigned, students read the course
textbook and come to class with their own ideas about how they
can incorporate that particular topic into their group's lesson plan.
After a class discussion of each topic, each lesson-planning group
meets to pool their ideas, modify their lesson plan, and identify additional resources they need. As part of this process, they consider
which learning theory-based instructional practices they will use.

As students develop their lessons, we expect them to justify
each step by using one or more reasons shown in Figure 3.5. Not
all reasons listed, however, need to be addressed in one lesson.

Resources for Problem 2

Cooperation is needed from the videotaped teacher who
needs to be willing to visit the college class. The teacher also needs

---

Figure 3.5

REASONS FOR INCLUDING EACH STEP IN THE LESSON PLAN

1. Content objective or purpose for learning content.
2. Thinking objective or purpose for learning thinking skill.
3. Attention-getter.
4. Recall of prior knowledge.
5. Attempt to ease working memory.
6. Effort to help students encode information (not just telling them).
7. Effort to teach a thinking skill.
8. Metacognition.
9. Transfer.
10. Assessment of objective.
11. Classroom management.
12. Direct instruction method suggested by Skinner.
13. Modeling method suggested by Bandura.
14. Radical constructivism method suggested by Piaget.
15. Social constructivism method suggested by Vygotsky.
16. Multiple intelligence used for problem solving other than verbal/linguistic or logical/math.
17. Motivation to increase self-efficacy.
18. Motivation to create disequilibrium.
19. Motivation to increase expectation of success.
20. Motivation to increase effort attributions.
21. Motivation to increase learning-goal orientation.
22. Motivation to increase self-determination.
23. Learner-centered practice.

Note: For an overview of the methods suggested in the figure, see Eggen & Kauchak, 1999.

to be accessible to share materials and answer questions by telephone. The principal needs to give permission for hiring a substitute teacher on the day when the teacher meets with the university students. This is a contribution of the public school.

The students need to obtain library or Internet resources and materials for their lesson plans. These may be provided from the teacher's school, requested from children's parents, borrowed from classmates, or even purchased by the university students. For example, students presenting a lesson on recycling provided garbage and plastic gloves. Students teaching the cardinal directions might purchase inexpensive compasses for each child or use those already in the school.

If student groups choose to present their lesson to the elementary school class, they must make their own transportation arrangements to get to the school. Because the trip is voluntary and not a course requirement, and because the lessons are scheduled at various times throughout the day, students must assume responsibility for their safety; no bus is hired. Undergraduates may also need permission to miss other classes that are regularly scheduled at the time when they are scheduled to present their lesson.

Requirements for Problem 2

To obtain enough information to solve Problem 2, students must complete assigned readings and attend class discussions on objectives, methods of encoding, thinking skills, motivation, transfer and assessment, and class management. They are also required to complete the following assignments related to their lesson:

- Create behavioral and cognitive objectives.
- Consider ways of encoding information for their lesson.
- Develop ways to prompt students to think metacognitively.
- Compare and evaluate applications of motivation theories.
- Identify benefits of various procedures for class management and choose appropriate ones.
- List the steps of their lesson and justify the steps.
- Choose an appropriate assessment and consider whether that assessment is measuring their objectives.
- Reflect on the strengths and weaknesses of the lesson after they present it to the entire class and at the elementary school.

Planning the lesson is clearly a major focus of the course. After presenting the lesson, groups also spend much time reflecting on such topics as how one part of the lesson affected other parts; how to use feedback from classmates who role-played students learning the lesson; why various elements were or were not included (and why they perhaps should have been included); how effective the lesson was; and what students would do differently if they presented the lesson again. Figure 3.6 offers questions to guide students in their reflections.

Figure 3.6
QUESTIONS TO GUIDE REFLECTION ON THE LESSON

Topic	Questions
Purpose for Learning	Did you share your objectives with the students you were teaching? If not, why not? Why are objectives important? Did you *tell* the students why they were learning the information in your lesson? If not, did you *ask* the students to share what they would get out of learning the information? If neither you nor the students set a purpose for learning, why not? Why is setting a purpose for learning important?
Attention	Did you *capture* their attention? Did you *keep* their attention? If not, what would you do differently?
Learner-Centered Focus	Was the lesson appropriate for most of the students at the age level? If not, was it too easy or too hard? Was the lesson related to the students' interests? How do you know? Did you build on the students' knowledge? If yes, how do you know? If no, why not? Why *should* you build on prior knowledge?
Thinking Skills	Did you discuss metacognition with the students? If not, why not? Why should the students discuss metacognition?
Assessment	Did you assess student learning and performance? If not, why not? If yes, was your assessment in line with your objectives? Was your assessment authentic? If yes, how do you know? Why *should* it be authentic? Did the students achieve your objectives? Which ones did they achieve? Which ones did they not achieve? Which ones do you not know whether they achieved? Did you teach or assess for transfer? If not, why not? Why is transfer important?
Anticipation of Problems	Did you have enough time? If there was too much time, did you have plans for what to do with the extra time? Were there any problems that you *had* anticipated? Describe what happened. Were there any problems that you had *not* anticipated? Describe what happened.
Evaluation	What worked best about your lesson? What would you change if you did it again?

Instructor's Role

For Problem 1, we videotape the class during the first month of the course. Our preparation includes negotiating a date for videotaping, arranging for the principal and parents to give permission for the children to be videotaped and for the tape to be shown to the educational psychology students, and obtaining equipment. During Weeks 4 and 5 of the course, we visit the elementary class to videotape a full day. Two people are needed: If two cameras are used, each operates a camera; if one camera is used, one person directs the cameraperson on what to videotape. Within the next two weeks, we edit the footage to create a 40- to 60-minute tape. Finally, we serve as liaisons with the teacher—delivering class questions to her through e-mail, collecting her answers, sharing them with the groups that posed the questions, and arranging for the teacher to visit the university class.

For Problem 2, we ask the elementary class teacher to suggest topics for lessons that the undergraduates can present on a particular date later in the semester. We also organize students into groups according to their lesson choices, and we arrange for the teacher to meet with them to answer initial questions about the students' prior knowledge. During the month before the students present their lessons, we create various assignments to provide needed background information and to promote thought about elements that the students could integrate into their lessons. In class, as soon as each element (e.g., objectives and methods encoding) is discussed, the lesson-planning groups meet to pool their ideas based on the assignments they have completed. At this time, we act as guides, consulting with each group. The groups submit their evolving plans, and we respond to and challenge their individual and collective ideas.

If a group chooses to present its lesson to the elementary school class and wants us present, we attend. But if a group believes that a visit by the instructor would be too stressful when presenting their first lesson, we honor their feelings. The classroom teacher is present throughout the lessons.

Assessment

Assessment is both formative and summative. Although we do not evaluate the actual delivery of the lesson, we review students' individual and group plans and ask them to revise until they demonstrate an understanding of and consideration for each of the major lesson topics. When all parts of an assignment are accurate, logical, and complete, the student receives passing credit for that part of the project. Grades are based on the number and types of assignments completed in the course. To earn a *C*, students must pass all PBL assignments. They can earn an *A* or a *B* by completing additional projects, such as reviewing Web sites and creating a journal.

Outcomes

We note outcomes in three general areas: evaluating plans for lessons, learner-centered beliefs, and the PBL experience. Students' plans for and reflections about lessons are evaluated through a series of course assignments. Learner-centered beliefs are evaluated through Likert questions (i.e., strongly agree, agree, disagree, and strongly disagree). The PBL experience is evaluated through responses to open-ended questions.

Lesson Plans

Each lesson is unique because each group has defined and approached its task differently, within general guidelines. For instance, one group designed a math "jeopardy" game. A different lesson asked students to explain their reasons for classifying an animal as endangered or not; another lesson coached children to form a matrix comparing and contrasting midwestern states. Groups are not required to include all the elements listed in Figures 3.5 and 3.6, but group members are expected to be able to justify their reasons for excluding parts.

PBL and Learner-Centered Beliefs

We are also interested in assessing the effect of PBL on students' learner-centered educational beliefs. Therefore, we ask them to take a beliefs survey twice: on the first day of the course and then again during the last week of classes. A survey of learner-centered beliefs developed by McCombs and Lauer (1997) distinguishes between learner-centered beliefs and nonlearner-centered beliefs about learners and teaching. Learner-centered teachers are characterized more by their low nonlearner-centered belief scores than by their high learner-centered belief scores relative to other teachers. For example, many teachers readily agree with the learner-centered belief, "Students achieve more in classes in which teachers encourage them to express their personal beliefs and feelings." There is far less agreement, however, about nonlearner-centered beliefs such as, "Students just want to be coddled" and "Innate ability is fairly fixed, and some children just can't learn as well as others." Results from the pre-PBL and post-PBL beliefs survey show that, over the course of a semester, the undergraduate students' learner-centered beliefs increased significantly, as well as the difference between their learner-centered and nonlearner-centered beliefs.

The learner-centered nature of the PBL practices is also confirmed when students evaluate their professors using an assessment developed by McCombs and Pierce (1999). The instrument assesses such practices as honoring student voice and encouraging higher-order thinking skills. Evaluations have been significantly higher than ratings of a general sample of undergraduate professors.

Evaluating PBL Experiences

When we ask them to evaluate their PBL experiences, undergraduates comment on the process of solving messy problems: "It requires patience, perseverance, and genuine acceptance and caring"; "I've learned that it is a step-by-step process that is not going to be solved all of a sudden. Much observation and application of ideas are needed to meet special needs." When asked about the role of teachers as problem solvers, one student observed, "They may not solve every problem, but it is their #1 job to pay close attention to the students and respond to individual needs."

Problems

We encountered several problems with PBL. One is the large amount of time students need to solve PBL problems. Requiring students to meet in groups outside class is not an option because their schedules do not usually permit it. Furthermore, the instructor can be held accountable for the safety of group members who are required to meet off campus. Although these problems might be addressed with a class electronic listserver, we have not found that option necessary. Instructors who are responsible for teaching a large amount of material to prepare students for certification should allow a sufficient amount of class time for students to solve the type of messy, ill-defined problems that occur with PBL.

Another problem is the time and effort the instructor needs to develop the problem and then second-guess the kinds of information that students will need and request in the process of trying to solve the problem.

Finally, initial experiences with PBL can be met with resistance from students who feel confused because they are unaccustomed to the demands of self-regulated problem solving that PBL requires.

Suggestions and Conclusions

The approach to PBL we describe offers one means of addressing the problems mentioned. The emphasis on individual mastery of objectives ensures that students demonstrate proficiency in the process and in the content addressed. Using matrices to represent information and working on related assignments enable students to learn how to structure their decision making efficiently and effectively. Thus, conveying large amounts of information is feasible. The graphic organizers and assignments provide structure and support as students define the problem from a variety of perspectives, sort and put in order of priority their information needs, and keep all data in mind while evaluating possible solutions. These assignments allow an efficient use of class time while presenting the scaffolding needed for those unfamiliar with self-regulated problem solving.

The large amount of time the instructor invests in PBL is still a concern. Although observing a videotaped real classroom provides an endless supply of authentic problems and supporting materials, the time saved in creating a problem and materials is spent in filming and editing the tape and in facilitating communication between the teacher and the undergraduates. To spend the time, one must believe that authenticity is extremely valuable.

REFERENCES

Alexander, P. A., & Murphy, P. K. (1998). The research base for the American Psychological Association's learner-centered psychological principles. In N. M. Lambert and B. L. McCombs (Eds.), *How students learn: Reforming schools through learner-centered education.* Washington, DC: American Psychological Association.
 A chapter presenting a compelling review of research that supports learner-centered principles.

American Psychological Association. (1997, November). *Learner-centered psychological principles: A framework for school redesign and reform* [Online]. Available: http://www.apa.org/ed/lcp.html (2000, November 28).
 A Web site listing and discussing the learner-centered principles.

Association for Childhood Education International. (2000). [Web site]. Available: http://www.udel.edu/bateman/acei/index.html (2000, November 21).
 This association is responsible for the program review process, within the National Council for the Accreditation of Teacher Education, for institutions seeking national accreditation in elementary education. This Web site includes the standards used.

Eggen, P., & Kauchak, D. (1999). *Educational psychology: Windows on classrooms* (4th ed.). Upper Saddle River, NJ: Merrill.
 A basic textbook used in educational psychology courses.

McCombs, B. L., & Lauer, P. A. (1997). Development and validation of the learner-centered battery: Self-assessment tools for teacher reflection and professional development. *The Professional Educator, 20*(1), 1–21.

An article describing surveys that can be used to assess learner-centered beliefs and practices.

McCombs, B. L., & Pierce, J. W. (1999). *The assessment of learner-centered practices (ALCP): Postsecondary level student survey (college level).* Unpublished manuscript available upon request from Dr. Barbara L. McCombs, Senior Research Scientist, Human Motivation, Learning, and Development, University of Denver's Research Institute, 2050 E. Iliff Avenue, Room 224, Denver, CO 80208-2616.

An instrument developed for students' evaluations of an instructor's learner-centered practices in higher education. Students also evaluate the motivation they experienced in the instructor's course.

Pierce, J., & Jones, B. (February, 1999). Problem-based learning: Learning and teaching in the context of problems. In S. Sears and J. DeStefano (Eds.), *Contextual teaching and learning: Preparing teachers to enhance student success in the work place and the world.* ERIC Clearing House in Adult Career and Vocational Education and ERIC Clearing House in Teaching and Teacher Education.

A chapter describing a research base for PBL and discussing how PBL is related to contextualized learning in teacher education.

4 The Inclusion Classroom Problem: Learning About Students with Disabilities

Katherine L. Hibbard, Barbara B. Levin, and Tracy C. Rock

As more students with disabilities are included in the general education classroom, preservice teachers need to develop knowledge, skills, and attitudes to teach students with a wide variety of special needs, including students with disabilities. In this chapter, we discuss how we used a problem-based learning (PBL) unit—the Inclusion Classroom—to provide these teachers with insight into an actual inclusion classroom. The unit is based on the actual experiences of a 2nd grade teacher. Working in pairs and small, cooperative learning groups, participants researched ways to include students with disabilities in a general education classroom and learned the importance of collaborating with other professionals to acquire a knowledge base about educating these children.

Context for PBL

We presented the PBL unit on the inclusion classroom to two cohorts of undergraduate elementary education majors during the second semester of a four-semester teacher education program at the University of North Carolina at Greensboro. The problem was part of the curriculum for a two-hour weekly seminar focused on learning to teach students with disabilities. The preservice teachers also spent 10 hours a week as interns in general education class-rooms in Professional Development Schools (PDSs) throughout the semester. Professional Development Schools work collabora-tively with universities to improve practices and understanding in four major areas: teacher education, professional development, student learning, and inquiry (Abdal-Haqq, 1998; Teitel, 1998). When we planned the PBL unit, we thought it would take only a portion of the semester to complete. What we discovered was that the problem became a reference point for most of the assignments and activities throughout the entire semester.

Purposes for Using PBL

We developed the PBL unit to provide a variety of opportuni-ties for our preservice teachers to explore issues related to teach-ing students with disabilities in a general education classroom. We also identified six broad goals that we wanted to achieve, and we aligned our goals with six of the 10 standards of the Interstate New Teacher Assessment and Support Consortium (INTASC) (1995). The standards specify what beginning teachers should know and be able to do. Here are our goals; related INTASC standards are shown in parentheses:

• Define various disabilities that students in public schools may be identified with today (Standard 2, Student Development).

• Understand the responsibilities of the general education teacher in developing and implementing individualized education programs (IEPs) for children with disabilities in their classrooms (Standard 8, Assessment).

• Learn a process for collaborating and working with special education teachers and other professionals in inclusive settings (Standard 10, School and Community Involvement).

• Identify specific strategies for teaching curriculum content to children with disabilities (Standard 3, Diverse Learners; Stan-dard 4, Multiple Instructional Strategies).

Figure 4.1

Problem: The Inclusion Classroom

You have been asked to teach a full-inclusion class of 18 2nd graders next year. The class will be small because several of your students have identified disabilities or other special needs. You will have the full support of the special education teacher; some of the children have full-time or part-time personal assistants. Of course, your trusted teacher's assistant will also be with you full time, and you may have a university intern if you want one. The class roster contains information about the class. You need to read it carefully and think about what you need to know before you say yes or no to taking on this special class. You may certainly talk it over with your peers and family members as you decide, but remember—someone has to teach this class, and your principal thinks you can do a good job.

Note: This problem is available at http://www.uncg.edu/~bblevin/ecpbl/ecpblproblem.html.

• Develop positive attitudes about including students with disabilities in the general education classroom (Standard 3, Diverse Learners).

• Develop skills in using a strengths-based approach to assess students' abilities and needs (Standard 7, Planning).

Students used research, interviews, field trips, guest speakers, directed readings, and observations or internships in inclusion classrooms to gather information on the problem.

Description of the PBL Assignment

We presented the PBL problem (Figure 4.1) and the class roster (Figure 4.2) to our students early in the semester. This problem described not only a real classroom in a nearby school district but also the dilemma that a recent graduate of our teacher education program faced after only two years of teaching: Should she accept the principal's offer to teach the full-inclusion class? After reading the problem and the class roster descriptions, students immediately began asking about the terms and acronyms that described the children.

Figure 4.2
CLASS ROSTER FOR THE INCLUSION CLASSROOM

Student's Name	Description
Sally Anderson	Sally is a young 7-year-old with average ability. She reads on grade level but is weak in math. Sally is the youngest member of her single-parent family. Her mother works in a factory.
Chris Block	Chris, age 8, has identified learning disabilities, which his IEP lists as auditory processing problems and dyslexia. He reads and writes at a preprimer level but is good in math. Chris's parents both work in white-collar jobs.
Christy Conner	Christy is a 7½-year-old who excels in spelling, writing, reading, and talking. She has some problems with math, but her parents are willing to help her at home.
Billy Eckstein	Billy is an 8-year-old with specific learning disabilities and a diagnosis of ADHD. His IEP discusses auditory memory problems and problems with sequencing, organization, and math. He is taking Ritalin, although his parents were reluctant to allow this medication.
Felicia Escobar	Felicia is a bright 7-year-old. Although she speaks excellent English and understands Spanish, Felicia does not like to speak Spanish at home or school. Her parents are bilingual and own a restaurant.
Antoine Fisher	Antoine is an articulate 7½-year-old who loves to read about science-related things. He always has his nose in a book and lives with his grandmother and older brother.
Brett Fundy	Brett is a 9-year-old with mild Down syndrome and is classified as EMD. His IQ is about 70, and his social skills are age appropriate for 2nd grade. His speech is difficult to understand, however, and he does not read or write. He will receive speech therapy, OT, and PT every week. Brett is new to this school.
Patty Gallagher	Patty is a 10-year-old with a low IQ and is identified as TMD. Patty is big for her age and prone to petit mal seizures. She can dress and feed herself and has the social skills of a 5-year-old. Her academic skills are low. Patty has been in our inclusion program for one year and lives with her mother, who is a nurse.
Pam MacDonald	Pam is also identified as TMD. She is 9 years old but is small for her age. Her social skills are coming along nicely, and she is able to feed and dress herself and use the bathroom. Pam lives with an experienced and caring foster family who has other children with disabilities.
Jenny Moore	Jenny is an above-average 7½-year-old who loves school. Her reading and math skills are on grade level. Her parents are both teachers.
Molly Olson	Molly is 8 and repeating 2nd grade because she was sick so much last year. She contracted meningitis and missed over two months of school. Until she got sick, Molly was doing fine in 2nd grade, and we think that will continue to be the case. Her parents are supportive, and her mother often volunteers at the school.

(continued)

	Figure 4.2
	—continued—
Sean O'Toole	Sean will soon turn 7. His social skills are not quite up to his above-average cognitive skills, but he interacts well in the classroom. He sometimes gets in trouble on the bus and the playground. His parents are recently divorced, and he lives with his mom; his older brother lives with his dad.
Emily Poole	Emily is 8 years old and has an 80 percent hearing loss from a high fever contracted when she was a toddler. Emily wears hearing aids and has some speech problems. You will have to wear an auditory trainer. Emily will go to speech therapy and may have an interpreter for part of the time. Emily's younger brother is also in this class. Emily's parents are pleased that she is in this inclusion classroom, and her mother often volunteers at the school.
Greg Poole	Greg is an average 7-year-old with grade-level skills in math and reading. He and Emily are siblings. Greg can use ASL and may be of help communicating with Emily.
Kristin Smith	Kristin is an average $7\frac{1}{2}$-year-old who is also working on grade level. Her parents are Jehovah's Witnesses and active with their church and Amway business.
Terry Smothers	Terry is an 8-year-old boy with cerebral palsy. He will have a personal assistant (PA) who is to be hired as soon as possible. The PA will help Terry use the bathroom and transfer into and out of his wheelchair to his desk or other special furniture. The PA will also assist Terry in the lunchroom and can help him with his work because Terry cannot control a pencil well enough to write. Everyone knows Terry at our school because he has been here since kindergarten. Although he repeated 1st grade, we feel he is ready to go on to 2nd grade this year. Terry's father is a doctor, and his mother was a nurse. She is now a stay-at-home mother.
Ellen Tracy	Ellen is a 7-year-old with good skills in reading and math. She is good friends with Emily and is learning ASL. Emily is the oldest of five children. Her dad is a minister.
Bobby Weeks	Bobby is new to our school this year. His cumulative folder indicates that he was an above-average student in his previous school. We don't know anything about the family at this time.

Student Names. All student names are pseudonyms. The descriptions are composites and do not describe actual children.

Guide to Abbreviations. The abbreviations are those commonly used in North Carolina. IEP: individual education program; ADHD: attention deficit/hyperactivity disorder; EMD: educably mentally disabled; OT: occupational therapy; PT: physical therapy; TMD: trainable mentally disabled; and ASL: American sign language. The abbreviations and terminology can be changed to reflect what is used in other locations.

We discussed the purpose of PBL, explaining that they would need to do some research to find answers to their questions about the children in this class. We gave them an opportunity to make

---

Figure 4.3
YOUR INITIAL RESPONSE TO THE PBL PROBLEM

You have just received the Inclusion Classroom PBL problem. Read through the scenario a couple of times. Think about your first thoughts and reactions as you prepare a written response to these questions:

- What is your initial response to the principal's request to take this teaching position? Be as detailed as possible—you might include your first reactions, gut feelings, emotions, concerns, and hopes.
- What do you need to know to make an informed decision about the request? What do you need to learn to make that decision?

---

notes about the questions they had and then asked them to write their initial response to this job offer (see Figure 4.3). They were given one week to turn in their response.

When we reviewed the responses, we noted that almost every preservice teacher wanted to learn more about the students with disabilities and the acronyms included in the student descriptions. We shared this finding with the students and asked them to form work groups to study the disabilities they had identified in their responses. We gave the groups guidelines for their research (Figure 4.4 on p. 62) and provided class time to develop a work plan. They presented their summaries to their groups during one seminar session near the end of the semester.

Over the course of the semester, the preservice teachers also participated in related activities to learn more about inclusive education, disabilities, other professionals working in the schools, and strengths-based approaches. Such activities included observing or interning in inclusive classrooms, keeping a reflective journal, interviewing a professional or paraprofessional, and observing a child with disabilities.

Observations or Internships in Inclusive Classrooms

The course requirements included a 10-hour per week internship in an elementary classroom. For one cohort, several internship placements were available in inclusion classrooms with

---

Figure 4.4
GROUP GUIDELINES FOR STUDYING DISABILITIES

In your PBL group, divide the disability areas you need to research evenly among the members. Each member should have two students with disabilities to research. Use the guidelines below to prepare a written summary of your research. Give the summary to your group when you share what you've learned on [date].

1. For each disability area, describe
   - Characteristics of the disability in school-age children.
   - Types of accommodations that may be appropriate for children with this disability.
   - Supports that are available to general education teachers who have a child with this disability in their classroom.

2. Design a specific set of strategies and accommodations that you would use with two students with disabilities you have researched who need help with reading, writing, or math.

---

students who had a variety of disabilities. For students in both cohorts who could not be placed in inclusion classrooms, arrangements were made for them to spend several hours observing in inclusion classrooms. Students were able to talk with teachers and teaching assistants during or after the observations. Some of the students observed in the actual classroom where the PBL problem was developed. The purpose of these site-based experiences was to give students the opportunity to see firsthand an inclusive classroom, to talk with staff about the benefits and challenges of such a situation, and to talk with the children in the classroom.

A Reflective Journal for *The Acorn People*

Early in the semester, we read and discussed *The Acorn People* by Ron Jones (1976). This memoir describes the author's experience as a counselor at a summer camp for children with multiple disabilities. As part of their biweekly journaling requirements, students were asked to keep a reflective journal as they read the book; Figure 4.5 shows the guiding questions they used. The purpose of this assignment was to help students see the possibilities and strengths that individual children with disabilities bring to a classroom—part of our goal of helping students develop positive attitudes.

Figure 4.5
GUIDING QUESTIONS FOR A REFLECTIVE JOURNAL ON
THE ACORN PEOPLE

1. Pick one of the children from the story. What are that child's strengths? How could you use those strengths in your classroom?

2. How did the mood change when the children were getting ready to go home from camp? Why do you think that happened?

3. What have you learned from this book about people who have disabilities? How might what you have learned affect what you do in your classroom?

Interview with a Professional or Paraprofessional

Students identified professionals other than classroom teachers who worked with students with disabilities in the schools. Pairs of students interviewed one person: school nurse, school counselor, special education teacher, special education assistant, school psychologist, social worker, physical therapist, occupational therapist, adaptive physical education teacher, or speech/language therapist. Some professionals were school district employees; others were staff from local service agencies who worked with a student and the student's family. To help students develop interview questions, we gave them specific content topics to focus on (discussed later in the chapter).

After the interview, each pair made a class presentation in which they summarized their findings. We encouraged them to include examples or minidemonstrations. Each pair also developed a one-page handout that highlighted the key points about the professional's roles and responsibilities and the process used for obtaining services.

These interviews helped our students understand the value of collaboration and the wide range of human resources available to classroom teachers. They also helped these preservice teachers begin to understand their role in the referral process and to see

---

Figure 4.6
QUESTIONS TO GUIDE CHILD OBSERVATION ACTIVITY

Watch the child in class. How does the child participate?
Look at the child's work. What types of assignments is the child doing?
Did the teacher make any modifications or adaptations?
Watch the child. What is the child's attention span and organization?
What types of questions does the child ask? Answer?
What are the child's interests? Hobbies?
Think about what you've learned about this child. What surprised you? How might what you've learned from this observation help you as an intern and as a teacher?

---

how the school is involved with the community to provide a full range of services for students with disabilities.

Observing a Child with Disabilities

Students observed a child with disabilities for several hours at their regular internship sites, using the questions shown in Figure 4.6 to guide their thinking. This activity built on a child-study project they had completed the previous semester. In that project, they observed a typically developing child for several hours and wrote a brief case study profile of the child. After observing and talking to the child with disabilities to learn about the child's interests, the students wrote about their experiences and what they learned. We then had a seminar discussion that focused on using a child's strengths and interests as the basis for lesson planning. This activity was geared toward our goals of developing skills in using a strengths-based approach toward assessment and developing positive attitudes about including students with disabilities in a general education classroom.

Expanded Learning Opportunities

In addition to the activities described earlier, students also participated in disability simulations (e.g., video simulations of learning disabilities [see Lavoie, 1989]), visited local agencies that provide services to people with disabilities, and contacted families

---

Figure 4.7
GUIDELINES FOR THE FINAL DECISION PAPER

Revisit the initial problem posed to you at the beginning of the semester. Write a two- to three-page paper describing your final decision about the principal's offer. Include this information:

- Issues you considered when making your decision.
- Descriptions of the activities that helped you make your decision.
- A list of questions or concerns you still have.

---

of children and adults with disabilities. Guest speakers included adults with developmental disabilities (e.g., mental retardation); staff from a local business that employs people with visual impairments; and school personnel, including the student assistance team chairperson and a special education teacher assistant. We also used several Web sites and print media as resources (see listing at the end of the chapter). These activities were designed to achieve our goals of developing positive attitudes about inclusion, understanding the general education teacher's role in IEP development and implementation, learning about collaboration, and learning about various disabilities.

Final Decision

For the last PBL assignment of the semester, we asked students to write a final decision paper about the principal's offer to teach the class described in the problem. Figure 4.7 shows the guidelines the students used.

Instructor's Role

We developed the problem and generated activities and assignments to further the students' learning. Our role was also to help students locate on-campus and community-based resources so that they could gather the information they needed to make an informed decision. Such work included scheduling time for classes to use a technology classroom on campus to access Internet sites and arranging for guest speakers. Students were given time in class to make presentations and discuss disability-related issues. We worked with local schools to provide students with opportunities to observe in inclusive classrooms.

Communicating through e-mail, students submitted reflective journals every two weeks, and we responded. We provided written feedback on all assignments and whole-group presentations. During internship visits and supervisory conferences, we were available to help the preservice teachers plan for students with special learning needs.

Assessment

In evaluating our students' disability studies, we checked to see if the written information about each disability was accurate and if the suggested modifications and accommodations were appropriate. We also assessed the quality of the students' writing (e.g., grammar and spelling). One cohort leader, whose background was not in special education, found it necessary to consult with other department members when she evaluated students' responses for content accuracy. In future semesters, to assist other cohort leaders whose areas of expertise do not include special education, we hope to have available sample answers to the kinds of disabilities our students identified and researched in their work plans.

We used a checklist to assess how well student pairs presented information on their interviews with a professional or paraprofessional. Figure 4.8 shows the checklist, which separates a presentation into seven topics. Along with our own evaluations, we asked several students to conduct peer evaluations of the presentation using the same checklist. Such work provided not only additional feedback to the presenters but also practice using checklists for the student evaluators.

Outcomes

As part of our ongoing evaluation of our undergraduate teacher education program, we administered a pre- and post-PBL

Figure 4.8
CHECKLIST FOR ASSESSING AN INTERVIEW PRESENTATION

Names of Two Presenters: _____

Profession Presented: _____

Topic Described	QUALITY OF PRESENTATION		
	Needs Work	Adequate	Excellent
Content of Presentation			
Job Description and Responsibilities			
Nature of Work with Classroom Teacher			
Education and Training Required for Job			
Referral Process for Identifying Students Needing Services			
Nature of Job in Five Years			
Mechanics			
Communication (e.g., flow, clarity, speaking volume and rate, and confidence)			
Written Handout (e.g., grammar and spelling)			

Comments:

---

beliefs survey about the practice of inclusion (Bailey & Winton, 1987). We administered the same survey a third time—at the end of the preservice teachers' student teaching semester, which occurred one year after completing the PBL semester. We found that positive beliefs about including children with disabilities in the general education classroom increased significantly for both cohorts of elementary education majors.

In the follow-up survey (one year after the PBL semester), the cohort of students who continued to have internship experiences and a semester of student teaching in inclusive settings showed additional increases in positive beliefs about inclusion. The cohort of students who did not have additional opportunities to intern in inclusive classrooms showed decreases from the post-PBL scores, though their scores remained higher than the pre-PBL scores (Hibbard, 1999).

When we analyzed the students' final decision papers on the PBL problem, we found that two activities were cited most often as contributing to their decisions: research and study of disabilities conducted on the topics they chose to learn more about, and observations or internships in inclusion classrooms. Students identified other activities as contributing to their learning, including talking with an inclusion teacher, interviewing other professionals, and receiving information from peers about the disabilities (Levin, Hibbard, & Rock, 1998). Their final papers provided useful feedback about activities that were meaningful for our students and gave us guidance for refining the PBL unit.

We also found that most students wrote about and included parts of their PBL activities in their INTASC-based teaching portfolios, which they completed by the end of their student teaching (one year after the PBL semester). Students made individual decisions about what artifacts to include to demonstrate competency for each INTASC standard. Selections from the PBL activities were seen in the standards dealing with collaboration with other professionals (Standard 10) and meeting students' individual needs (Standard 3).

Problems

A major challenge was providing opportunities for all students to spend time in inclusion classrooms. The PDS sites we work with offer a wide range of placement options for students with disabilities. But only one is an inclusion school where all students are educated in a general education classroom with numerous supports and services from professionals and paraprofessionals. The other PDS sites provide services in resource and self-contained classrooms. Although this situation limited the opportunities for all our preservice teachers to spend time in an inclusion classroom, it provided many occasions for discussing different service delivery options and the benefits and challenges each produced. Of course, those students who spent an entire semester interning in an inclusion classroom gained more knowledge and skills than those who were only able to observe for a limited time (Hibbard, 1999; Levin, Hibbard, & Rock, 1998).

Some students had difficulty setting up interviews with the itinerant professionals (e.g., occupational therapists) at their internship sites. Perhaps scheduling the interviews on days these type of professionals are regularly at the PDS site or at their home base school would help solve this problem. Because the students identified the interviews as important to their decision making, finding ways to keep the assignment as a required part of the PBL experience is important.

Suggestions and Conclusions

The PBL unit on inclusion enabled students to learn about children with disabilities. Using an authentic problem and class roster made the activities relevant; visiting the actual classroom of the teacher on whom the problem was based added to that relevancy.

The PBL problem lent itself well to a semester-long study. The learning opportunities were involved and required extensive study, observation, conversation, and self-reflection. We found that the related activities we included, although not designed specifically for the PBL problem, contributed to the students' decision-making process and understanding of the issues surrounding inclusion, including collaboration and accommodating students with disabilities. These expanded learning opportunities—disability simulations, guest speakers, field trips, and contact with adults with disabilities—added value and more of a lifespan perspective about disabilities.

Over the course of the semester, we identified several ways that we might change or fine-tune how we used the problem and the related activities. To help students become more skilled at self-directed learning, we could restructure the activities in which they use cooperative learning groups to study the disabilities. Rather than providing the degree of structure found in the Group Guidelines for Studying Disabilities (Figure 4.4 on p. 62), we could instead ask the groups to use their initial responses to the problem to develop both a series of questions related to the problem and a plan for finding answers to those questions. Their findings could be shared within the group and across groups in the cohort.

The students could also help develop an evaluation rubric for the presentation about the interviews they conducted with professionals who work with students with disabilities. Such a rubric would provide not only a more detailed tool than the checklist we used, but also an opportunity for students to practice developing rubrics.

Students began to develop the knowledge, skills, and attitudes they will need to successfully teach students with disabilities in general education classrooms. Assignments and activities helped them identify what they needed and wanted to learn about inclusion issues and to work in pairs and small groups to address those issues. Students learned that an array of other professionals is available to work with. The PBL unit proved to be a successful tool for our students to meet the goals of the semester-long course.

REFERENCES

Abdal-Haqq, I. (1998). *Professional Development Schools: Weighing the evidence.* Thousand Oaks, CA: Corwin.

    A book providing information on the background and current state of the Professional Development School movement in the United States.

Bailey, D., & Winton, P. (1987). *Benefits and drawbacks of early childhood inclusion.* Chapel Hill, NC: Frank Porter Graham Child Development Center.

    A book containing the inclusion beliefs survey used with the students who participated in the PBL problem in this chapter.

Hibbard, K. L. (1999). [Pre-, post-, and one-year follow-up results from an inclusion beliefs survey]. Unpublished raw data.

    A manuscript detailing the quantitative analysis of a survey about beliefs used with students who piloted the PBL unit discussed in this chapter.

Interstate New Teacher Assessment and Support Consortium. (1995). *Next steps: Moving toward performance-based licensure in teaching.* Washington, DC: Council of Chief State School Officers.

    A document detailing 10 competencies that beginning teachers should know and be able to do.

Jones, R. (1976). *The acorn people*. New York: Bantam/Doubleday.

An easy-to-read book based on the author's experience as a summer camp counselor for children with disabilities.

Lavoie, R. D. (1989). *How difficult can this be? The F.A.T. City workshop*. [Videotape]. (Available from PBS Home Video: 877-PBS-SHOP; http://www.pbs.org).

A videotape of a group of teachers, parents, students, and other interested community members participating in simulations of learning disabilities.

Levin, B. B., Hibbard, K. L., & Rock, T. C. (1998, October). *Exploring problem-based learning with undergraduate preservice teachers: A vehicle for instruction about inclusion*. Paper presented at the annual meeting of the American Association for Teaching and Curriculum, Orlando, FL.

A paper presenting the results of qualitative research on the effect of this PBL unit on changes in attitudes about inclusion from two pilot groups.

Teitel, L. (1998). *Governance: Designing Professional Development School governance structures*. Washington, DC: American Association for Teaching and Curriculum.

A document offering various examples of how Professional Development Schools should be organized.

ADDITIONAL RESOURCES

Academy for Educational Development. (n.d.). National Information Center for Children and Youth with Disabilities [Web page]. Available: http://www.nichcy.org (2000, September 21).

The center's Web site that includes information about disabilities, strategies for teachers to use in the classroom, information for parents, and other resources.

Bauwens, J., & Hourcade, J. J. (1997). Cooperative teaching: Pictures of possibilities. *Intervention in School and Clinic, 33*(2), 81–85, 89.

An article presenting descriptions of several team-teaching models. The diagrams of each model are helpful.

San Francisco School District (1997). *Collaborating for change: Including all of our students* [Videotape]. (Available from TSMedia Inc., 18 Halley Court, Fairfield, CT 06430; 800-876-6334).

A videotape of several inclusive classrooms (K–12). It includes conversations with faculty, administrators, parents, and students.

Turnbull, A., Turnbull, R., Shank, M., & Leal, D. (1999). *Exceptional lives: Special education in today's schools*. Upper Saddle River, NJ: Merrill.

A basic textbook that includes information about the history of special education and changes in inclusive practices, disabilities, and strategies for teachers.

University of North Carolina at Greensboro. (n.d.). Learning to meet the needs of Exceptional Children in an Inclusion Classroom [Web page]. Available: http://www.uncg.edu/~bblevin/ecpbl/ecpblproblem.html (2000, November 21).

The university's Web site that includes the PBL problem in this chapter and links to Internet resources on meeting the needs of exceptional children.

5 The Charter School and Problem-Based Learning

Barbara B. Levin

The charter school movement is growing and will affect teachers in many ways in the next 20 years. To help preservice teachers understand the issues surrounding charter schools, I developed a rich problem-based learning (PBL) unit that was offered toward the end of students' teacher preparation programs. Working in small, self-selected groups, students designed and defended a charter school proposal, revisiting and synthesizing all parts of their preparatory program. A mock school board of professors and administrators from the University of North Carolina at Greensboro evaluated their proposals and decided the fate of their charter school. This chapter describes the PBL unit I designed.

Context for PBL

A PBL unit to design a charter school was one of the major events in a summer course at the University of North Carolina at Greensboro. Entitled Elementary School Curriculum, the course was part of a 15-month, graduate-level program that led to a master's degree in curriculum and instruction and an initial teaching license.

The PBL unit took two weeks of the five-week course, allowing participants 15–18 hours of in-class time to read, conduct research, and meet with their PBL group. Their oral presentations to the mock school board occurred at the end of the unit, followed by additional debriefing and reflection. Although this course focused on concerns at the elementary school level, the PBL unit described in this chapter could easily be adapted to any school level.

Purposes for Using PBL

The overall goal of the unit was to engage preservice teachers in a process that would help them think deeply about all facets of the elementary school curriculum: student learning; best teaching practices; and purposes of other aspects of schooling, including school governance and organization, student assessment, parental involvement, school budgets, and facilities management. Working in small groups encouraged students to research, read, reflect on, discuss, and synthesize the multitude of factors that go into creating a school. The PBL unit provided a catalyst and focus for prospective teachers to review and rethink everything they had learned in their teacher education program.

To guide unit development, I selected specific objectives from the standards for elementary education program accreditation suggested by the National Center for the Accreditation of Teacher Education (NCATE), which were in place at the time. Although NCATE has revised its standards, here are the objectives that I used as student goals:

• Engage in experiences that exemplify various teacher roles, school organizations, and philosophical variants (e.g., essentialism, perrenialism, progressivism, constructivism, and existentialism).
• Understand the dynamics of curriculum change and school improvement through studying the role of elementary school teachers and professional organizations in curriculum development.
• Develop analytical and interpersonal skills essential for participating in curriculum change and school improvement.

Figure 5.1
PROBLEM: DESIGNING A CHARTER SCHOOL

Your elementary school has decided to convert into a charter school under North Carolina's new laws (House Bill 955, ratified on June 21, 1996). You are a nontenured teacher at this school, with two years of teaching experience. You have decided to participate in discussions about the goals and purposes of this new charter school before you decide whether or not to apply to teach there. Fifty percent of the teachers must agree to the charter school proposal for it to go forward. Will you stay or will you leave the school you will help design?

Note: This problem is available at http://www.uncg.edu/~bblevin/charterpbl/charterinstructions.html.

• Engage in activities that stimulate reflective and critical thinking, problem solving, and decision making within and across disciplines in the elementary school curriculum.

• Study and apply various models of curriculum theory and curriculum integration.

• Study and apply current research findings and best practices about teaching and learning to the elementary school curriculum.

Description of the PBL Assignment

During Week 3 of the five-week course, I introduced students to problem-based learning and presented the problem shown in Figure 5.1.

Resources

Resources included background information on charter schools, materials from a local education agency, and guest speakers knowledgeable about charter school proposals. Figure 5.2 (see p. 76) highlights pertinent North Carolina legislation as of June 1996.

I encouraged students to use the Internet to locate information on the charter school movement and on legislation in other states. Although every state's charter school legislation is different, the issues and procedures are similar, and because charter schools are

---

Figure 5.2
EXTRACT FROM CHARTER SCHOOL LEGISLATION IN NORTH CAROLINA
(JUNE 1996)

House Bill 955 [ratified June 21, 1996]: An act to increase educational opportunity by authorizing the creation and funding of charter schools, which are deregulated schools under public control.

§115C-238.29A. Purposes.

The purpose of this part is to authorize a system of charter schools to provide opportunities for teachers, parents, pupils, and community members to establish and maintain schools that operate independently of existing schools, as a method to accomplish the following:

1. Improve student learning.
2. Increase learning opportunities for all students, with special emphasis on expanded learning experiences for students who are identified as at risk of academic failure or academically gifted.
3. Encourage the use of different and innovative teaching methods.
4. Create new professional opportunities for teachers, including the opportunities to be responsible for the learning program at the school site.
5. Provide parents and students with expanded choices in the types of educational opportunities that are available within the public school system.
6. Hold the schools established under this part accountable for meeting measurable student achievement results, and provide the schools with a method to change from rule-based to performance-based accountability systems. (1995 [Reg. Sess., 1996], c. 731, s.2.

Note: Text is available at http://www.ncpublicschools.org/charter_schools/legislation.html.

---

public schools, this problem is relevant for all teachers. The PBL unit was especially relevant for the teachers who would be working in North Carolina because the charter school legislation in North Carolina was being refined in 1996, and the first charters were to be granted in 1997.

In 1996, our guest speaker was Frances F. Jones, former ASCD president and director of the Piedmont Triad Horizons Education Consortium in North Carolina. In 1997, Debbie Hill, a student in the 1996 class, spoke to the students. Hill is the author of a successful charter school proposal for Downtown Middle School in Winston-Salem, North Carolina, which opened in 1997.

Project Requirements

We discussed what the PBL problem and project requirements (Figure 5.3 on pp. 78–80) encompassed, what students would need to know to develop a charter school, and where they might find additional resources. They then gathered into seven self-selected groups of three to seven members. The invited speaker talked about her experience designing a charter school proposal, and students asked clarifying questions before going off to work in their groups.

For their final product, each group made a 20- to 30-minute oral presentation about their charter school. To enhance their presentation, we asked them to use a visual aid, such as a brochure or overhead transparencies; another option was to make a multi-media presentation.

Instructor's Role

Before the course began, I designed the PBL unit and assessment procedures. During the PBL unit, my role was to guide rather than serve as the source of knowledge or the information-giver (Delisle, 1997; Torp & Sage, 1998). I consulted regularly with each group to help them clarify the problem, consider additional resources, focus them on the tasks that needed to be accomplished, and help them move toward their deadlines. Regular class was suspended for four days so that groups could meet either on or off campus. During this time, I was available in person and through e-mail to answer queries.

In addition to designing the PBL unit, I developed a checklist to guide the oral presentations and recruited several university faculty and administrators to act as a mock state school board and review student proposals. Because the state school board grants charter schools in North Carolina, the mock board was as close to an authentic assessment task as we could get.

Figure 5.3
PROJECT REQUIREMENTS FOR THE CHARTER SCHOOL PROPOSAL

PART I. GROUP REQUIREMENTS

The North Carolina application for a charter school incorporates elements of an *educational plan* and a *business plan.* These two components are essential in providing a sound foundation to operate a charter school. As your group develops a proposal, include the elements outlined below.

Educational Plan

The education portion of the proposal should focus on describing the school's plan for addressing student learning.

Description and Background
- Brief mission statement—your philosophy or vision for the school. This statement should guide the rest of the proposal.
- Goals of the school program.
- School name.
- School setting—community and demographics.
- Type of school.
  - Size of proposed school population (staff and students).
  - Range of student ages and grades.
  - Description of target student population.
  - Hours and days of operation.
  - Description of the facility. Is it a new or converted building?
- Annual school calendar.
- Promise of the charter school: "This school promises to _____, and its charter can be revoked if_____."

Curriculum Framework
- Curriculum focus, philosophy, and scope.
- Content of the curriculum. What is the basis (e.g., North Carolina Standard Course of Study or national curriculum standards, such as those from the National Science Teachers Association, National Council for the Social Studies, and International Reading Association)?
- Structure of classes (e.g., self-contained, multi-age, and open).
- Classroom organization (e.g., desks, tables, team teaching, multi-age classes, looping, and inclusion).
- Instructional approaches (e.g., didactic, Paideia, and discovery).
- Other focuses (e.g., technology and community service).

Assessment Plans
- Expected student outcomes.
- Ways to evaluate student performance (e.g., North Carolina end-of-grade tests, national tests, performance-based assessments, and portfolios).

Staffing Requirements
- Desirable teacher traits.
- Teacher-student ratio.
- Percent of licensed teachers.

(continued)

Figure 5.3

—continued—

- Desirable administrator traits.
- Roles and responsibilities of teachers, support staff, and administrators.

Governance Structure and Policies
- Parent, family, and community involvement. Is it optional or required?
- Discipline plans.
- Administrative structure.
- Administrative roles.
- Educational approach and design, including admission and enrollment policies.
- Agreements with other agencies, if applicable.

Business Plan
The business portion of the proposal is essentially a small-business plan showing how the charter school can be economically viable. Creating a balanced budget is one of the most difficult tasks facing a charter school.

Budget
- Tentative first-year operating budget based on $4,400 per pupil.
  - Salaries.
  - Transportation.
  - Insurance.
  - Facilities expenses, including rent, mortgage, insurance, and utilities.
  - Instructional materials (e.g., supplies, books, and computer resources).
  - Food.
  - Contracted services (e.g., health and safety, psychological, and special education).
  - Other expenses.
- Tentative financial arrangements (e.g., grants, tuition, lab and technology fees, book rentals, and fund-raising events).

Potential Obstacles to Success
Examples include inability to acquire supplemental funding (e.g., grants, donations, and business partnerships); lack of available adequate facilities; weak community or parental support for mission of the school; not enough certified personnel; and excessive cost overruns.

Evidence of Effective Research
Attach all references used (e.g., print material, human resources, and Web-based resources).

PART II. INDIVIDUAL REQUIREMENTS
- Participate in doing research, attend all planning discussions, and have a role in the oral presentation.
- Write an essay about the promises and pitfalls of the group's proposal. Agree or disagree with the proposal; give your reasons and suggest alternatives.
- Write a statement explaining how you participated in the group and contributed to the project.

(continued)

Figure 5.3

—continued—

- Write a statement evaluating your experience in the group as you worked on the project.

PART III. GRADING

This PBL project accounts for 20 percent of your grade in the course. You will be evaluated on your participation in and contribution to group work. Half of your project grade (10 percent of the course grade) will be based on how well you addressed all the elements in Part I; the other half (10 percent of the course grade), on the individual written work described in Part II.

Assessment

To assess group presentations, the mock school board and randomly selected class members used a checklist to give feedback. I made notes and preliminary judgments on it. The original checklist proved to have too many areas to assess effectively during the 20- to 30-minute presentation. I subsequently developed two separate checklists—one for the oral presentation (Figure 5.4) and one for the written product (Figure 5.5 on p. 82)—and they worked better.

Before assigning final grades, I considered feedback from the evaluators who used the oral presentation checklist (Figure 5.4). I also used the written proposal checklist (Figure 5.5) to assess the content and quality of each group's proposal before determining a collective grade for the group. Individual grades were based on required essays and statements described in Part II of the original assignment (Figure 5.3).

The most helpful feedback came from the mock school board, the student audience, oral comments and questions the audience asked after each presentation, and notes the evaluators wrote on the checklists. Despite the feedback's usefulness, a majority of the students indicated that they found the school board to be intimidating, especially when board members questioned them about assessment plans for the charter school. Ironically, the students in this course were concurrently enrolled in a tests and measurement

	Figure 5.4		
	CHECKLIST FOR ASSESSING AN ORAL PRESENTATION ON A CHARTER SCHOOL		
Area and Criterion	**Needs Work (0–6 points)**	**Adequate (7–8 points)**	**High Quality (9–10 points)**
Educational Content of Presentation Covered all elements in the educational plan.			
Business Content of Presentation Covered all elements in the business plan.			
Effectiveness of Presentation Engaged audience interest.			
Pacing of Presentation Kept to time allotted.			
Potential Obstacles to Proposal's Success Shared explicitly.			
Quality of Visual Aids Added to understanding the proposal.			
Ability to Answer Audience and School Board Questions Demonstrated knowledge and understanding of issues.			
Evidence of Teamwork Included all members in presentation.			

course, but they had not made the connection between individual assessment of student knowledge and the ways a charter school might be held accountable for student performance. The area of accountability was a weak point in most of the presentations, but it provided good feedback for us about an area of our teacher education program that needed improvement.

Outcomes

I think that PBL fulfilled the NCATE objectives that served as goals for this course. Students engaged in experiences that allowed them to better understand various teacher roles and school organizations, and they applied the philosophical approaches they had

Figure 5.5
CHECKLIST FOR ASSESSING A WRITTEN PROPOSAL ON A CHARTER SCHOOL

Area	Needs Work (0–6 points)	Adequate (7–8 points)	High Quality (9–10 points)
Description and Background			
Curriculum Framework			
Assessment Plans			
Staffing Requirements			
Governance Structure and Policies			
Budget			
Potential Obstacles to Success			
Evidence of Effective Research			

Note to evaluator: Please refer to Project Requirements handout (Figure 5.3) to review specific items to be included for each area in Column 1.

learned in the first few weeks of the course to their charter school proposals. Most of the groups based their charter schools on constructivist theories of learning (Brooks & Brooks, 1993; Fosnot, 1995), which is the theory the teacher education program at the University of North Carolina at Greensboro is based on. Of course, other legitimate educational theories could serve equally as well.

Students also seemed to understand the dynamics of curriculum change and school improvement, shown by their written and oral comments throughout the PBL process. All participants used analytical and interpersonal skills, engaged in reflective and critical thinking, and employed problem-solving and decision-making skills within and across disciplines. Many had these skills before coming into the teacher education program, but the PBL unit reinforced and sharpened those skills as the students applied them to a new area.

The PBL unit allowed participants to apply various models of curriculum theory and integration that they had learned earlier in the course. As they designed their charter schools, they had multiple opportunities to apply current research findings and best practice about teaching and learning. In fact, one textbook for the course was *Best Practice: New Standards for Teaching and Learning in America's Schools* (Zemelman, Daniels, & Hyde, 1993).

From my perspective as the instructor, the PBL unit was an excellent learning experience for these prospective teachers. Anecdotal feedback from the mock school board and audience and the students' course evaluations supported my assessment.

Problems

In addition to needing to revise the grading checklists, I think the students would have benefitted from using true rubrics to guide their work. Using rubrics instead of simple checklists would have helped them better understand what I expected and what constituted "needs work," "adequate," and "high quality" for each criteria I was assessing in their oral and written presentations.

Several elements of the business plan were problematic—especially the budget. Although I had told students to spend 80–85 percent of their time on developing the educational plan and only 15–20 percent on the business plan and budget, the budget task raised the most questions and took more time than I had anticipated. Some groups had members with relevant background or work experience in finance, while other groups did not have such expertise. As a result, this part of the unit was frustrating for some groups, and not all were able to make their budgets realistic. Their recognition of what goes into planning a school, including the business side, was eye-opening for them.

Time was at a premium in this summer course, and all participants agreed that they could have used more time for doing research, discussing options, and reaching consensus about their education plan. Many individuals and groups spent more time on the unit out of class than they did in class (I had allotted 15–18 hours in class). Nevertheless, given the limited amount of time available, every group was ready for its oral presentation, and each group did a commendable job on a complex task.

The size of the groups, which were self-selected and varied from three to seven people, was problematic. Small groups (three to four students) found that reaching consensus and arranging their schedules to meet outside of class was easier, but their perspectives and ability to do extensive research were somewhat restricted. Large groups (five to seven students) needed more time to discuss the ideas that each member suggested and to share their research before reaching consensus on a plan. Groups with four to five members seemed optimal. Nevertheless, all groups worked well together, perhaps because they chose their own members and already knew each other from taking classes together for over a year.

Suggestions and Conclusions

Although the PBL unit on charter schools was successful, it would probably be even more successful during a semester-long course. Students would have more time between classes for research, reflection, and writing. This particular PBL project works best as a final experience in teacher education because it serves as a focus for teacher candidates to revisit and rethink everything they have read and experienced in their teacher preparation program. Because charter schools are frequently in the news, convincing the students that the issue was relevant was not difficult.

Bringing in school administrators with budget experience might have eliminated some frustration that many groups felt in completing the budget part of the problem. But my telling them that they did not have to spend a lot of time on the budget did not alleviate their concern or their desire to know more about this side of education. Despite their concerns, the budget element needed to be included to keep the problem authentic. Participants must struggle with the financial issues and learn that there are many aspects of schooling that may not be understood by beginning teachers.

If time had permitted, I would have engaged the class in designing full-blown rubrics for the unit, which would serve three purposes. First, the rubrics would force the participants to develop precise criteria for what constituted a high-quality mission statement or staffing proposal. Second, they would allow prospective teachers to gain experience in developing rubrics. Third, the rubrics would help students clarify what is important to accomplish as they worked on the assignment and prepared their oral presentations and written proposals.

I do not believe that every teacher education program needs to completely revamp its entire curriculum to engage students in PBL. One PBL activity, however, is probably not enough, and using only PBL experiences is overkill. Furthermore, teacher education faculty are knowledgeable about many good forms of pedagogy and are unlikely to teach in one way.

PBL can be used effectively for teacher education if the problems are designed carefully and placed selectively in the curriculum. Such experiences allow prospective teachers to engage with real-world problems that require them to find, evaluate, and use appropriate learning resources, just as they would expect their students to do. They need to experience the problems and the joys of working together effectively in groups before they can manage group work in their own classrooms. PBL provides authentic tasks for practicing oral and written communication skills, conducting research, applying information to new situations, and synthesizing what they have learned in their teacher education program.

REFERENCES

Brooks, M. G., & Brooks, J. G. (1993). *The case for the constructivist classroom.* Alexandria, VA: Association for Supervision and Curriculum Development.
    A popular book outlining the basis for creating classrooms based on constructivist theories of learning.

Delisle, R. (1997). *How to use problem-based learning in the classroom.* Alexandria, VA: Association for Supervision and Curriculum Development.
    A practical book detailing how to undertake PBL. It provides several examples of PBL units that can be used in K–12 settings.

Fosnot, C. T. (1995). *Constructivism: Theory, perspectives, and practice.* New York: Teachers College Press.

A book providing information about the theory, research, and practice called constructivism.

Torp, L., & Sage, S. (1998). *Problems as possibilities: Problem-based learning for K–12 education.* Alexandria, VA: Association for Supervision and Curriculum Development.

A book providing reasons that PBL works with students and examples of PBL in K–12 settings.

Zemelman, S., Daniels, H., & Hyde, A. (1993). *Best practice: New standards for teaching and learning in America's schools.* Portsmouth, NH: Heinemann.

A book summarizing principles and giving specific examples of best practices in literacy, science, mathematics, and social studies.

ADDITIONAL RESOURCES

Stepien, W. J., Gallagher, S. A., & Workman, D. (1993). Problem-based learning for traditional and interdisciplinary classrooms. *Journal for the Education of the Gifted, 16*(4), 338–357.

A research article detailing successful PBL activities in two secondary education courses.

University of North Carolina at Greensboro. (n.d.). Designing a charter school: A problem-based learning unit [Web site]. Available: http://www.uncg.edu/~bblevin/charterpbl/charterinstructions.html (2000, November 20).

The university's Web site that includes the PBL problem in this chapter and links to Internet resources on charter schools.

6 Using Problem-Based Learning to Teach Problem-Based Learning

SARA M. SAGE

AS WE LOOK TOWARD PREPARING OUR GRADUATES FOR A DIVERSE AND information-rich society in this century, we realize that our education students must possess the knowledge, skills, and dispositions to teach their own students in an increasingly complex world (Interstate New Teacher Assessment and Support Consortium, 1992). As teacher educators, we want to find teaching strategies that will help prepare our students for these tasks. Problem-based learning (PBL), which centers curriculum and instruction on a messy, authentic problem, is one such strategy (Torp & Sage, 1998). In this chapter, I present a brief sketch of a workshop in which I used PBL on multiple levels: as a teaching strategy for the course; as a modeling strategy for teachers taking the course; and as an outcome—class members designed PBL units to be used with their own students.

Context for PBL

The PBL workshop was offered as a graduate elective in the division of education at Indiana University South Bend. It was a three-credit course with a deferred grade arrangement (described later in the chapter). I taught the course in a one-week summer workshop (four and one-half days) open to graduate students in secondary education, elementary education, special education, counseling, and school leadership in either degree or certification programs. In this particular workshop, 14 graduate students took the class: four elementary school teachers, three middle school teachers, one principal, one special education teacher, one adult education instructor, one adjunct university faculty/secondary education major, two counseling students, and one speech therapist.

Purposes for Using PBL

Teacher education, as well as public education, has seen numerous reform efforts. Current reforms are remarkably similar: Most are grounded in an underlying cognitive or reflective theory of learning that states that teachers must think critically and reflectively about their own practice. Teaching is no longer seen as simply a set of learned skills, but rather as using teaching skills through a decision-making, problem-solving approach.

Discussion continues on the need for individual teachers to create their own unique understandings of the teaching and learning process, using the interaction of what they already know and believe, and the ideas and experiences with which they come into contact, as the basis (Richardson, 1997). This theory of learning as meaning making is called constructivism and is proposed as an undergirding set of propositions on which to base teacher education programs (Fosnot, 1989; Richardson, 1997).

One choice I have made as a teacher educator attempting to be a reflective—and constructivist—practitioner is to teach all my courses using a problem-solving orientation. In the workshop, I chose to combine reflection and teaching philosophy with real action by using problem-based learning. I taught class members how to use PBL in their own teaching situations, and I used PBL as the delivery method for the course.

PBL is certainly a timely topic (see, for example, Delisle, 1997; Torp & Sage, 1998), but it is not a strategy widely known or used in the schools in my area. Consequently, I believed that modeling the PBL approach was important (Sage & Torp, 1997). For the first day, I presented a short PBL experience that modeled both the design and the implementation of a PBL unit. The activity was also relevant for K–12 area students. For the remaining three and one-half days, course members worked on designing a PBL unit appropriate for their own teaching situations. Figure 6.1 (see p. 90) outlines the workshop's daily schedule.

Description of the PBL Assignments

Students had two PBL assignments. The first was the ill-structured problem they worked to solve the first day of the course. An ill-structured problem is one that is messy and has many possible answers. This problem, which I designed and called "Blowin' in the Wind," demonstrated how PBL might be used in the participants' own classrooms and modeled how to use local issues and current events as the basis for problems. Earlier that spring, a tornado had devastated a local mobile home park (and it just so happened that one class member's students had been affected). In this problem, students role-played members of a mobile home community who could be affected by severe weather. Figure 6.2 (see p. 91) gives the role and situation for the problem, and Figure 6.3 (see p. 92) presents the hook.

Using a blend of real issues—a real area mobile home park, print and online resources, and guests from the local emergency management agency—and a few created elements—fictitious park name and another student to role-play the assistant park manager—students worked in teams most of the day to investigate the problem and recommend a safety plan. Figure 6.4 (see p. 93) is a problem map showing the various areas of inquiry in the problem.

In the afternoon, students presented their results to the assistant park manager. I did not formally evaluate student presentations, but we discussed types of PBL assessments, including a sample rubric I had developed that could have been used (Figure 6.5 on p. 94). I used the experience to help students understand the PBL process inductively: Begin with the whole; break it down into details.

Figure 6.1
DAILY SCHEDULE FOR THE WORKSHOP

Half Day	Monday	Tuesday	Wednesday	Thursday	Friday
A.M.	Breakfast Introductions Begin "Blowin' in the Wind" PBL experience: Students meet the problem, identify what they know and need to know, develop the problem statement, and conduct inquiries.	See videotape on PBL. Begin design process: Who are my learners? Consider problem ideas and curriculum outcomes.	See videotape on PBL. Participate in minisessions with experienced PBL teachers. Participate in large-group synthesis discussion.	Coaching. Discuss how teachers implement PBL. Compare traditional vs. constructivist classrooms. Questioning: Conduct a minilecture on what questioning means. Questioning: Work on microteach activity in which learners practice questioning with each other.	Breakfast Discuss PBL resources. Discuss PBL implementation issues in your school. Share units with the class. Conduct final evaluations. Write Reflection Journal 5 (final workshop activity).
P.M.	Complete the PBL experience, determining and presenting solutions. Debrief the PBL experience. Discuss definition and parameters of PBL. Go over syllabus. Write Reflection Journal 1.	Learn about Inspiration® (software for mapping problem) in the computer lab. Consider role, situation, and a hook for the problem. Write Reflection Journal 2.	Learn about PBL assessments: authentic assessments for problems, formative and summative assessments, and rubrics. Work independently (mentored time). Write Reflection Journal 3.	Develop a problem plan. Work independently (mentored time). Write Reflection Journal 4.	

Figure 6.2
ROLE AND SITUATION FOR "BLOWIN' IN THE WIND" PROBLEM

Role: Students are a group of mobile homeowners in Fable Club Estates owned by Sales, Inc., in Anytown, Indiana.

Situation: The mobile homeowners are concerned about their safety in high winds and potential tornadic storms, given recent storms and tornadoes in the area that devastated several mobile home parks. The mobile home park currently has no shelter or office building. Should there be a shelter? What are other options for residents' safety? How high is the risk of potential damage? Are any actions necessary at this point? If actions are taken, what effect will they have on the residents? Representatives of the mobile home community have gathered for a partial day of discussion and investigation and will speak with the assistant manager of the park in the afternoon to share their concerns and give their recommendations.

The second PBL assignment was the heart of the course: Class members designed PBL units for their students. This work—as is a majority of any teacher's planning work—was also an ill-structured problem. The class members might have defined their problem for the week as, How can we as educators design a PBL unit for our own teaching situations in such a way that

- We consider the needs of our learners, curriculum, and classrooms.
- The problem will hook our students.
- The problem fits the critical parameters of PBL (such as ill-structuredness).
- We have our required design products completed by Friday and pass the course.
- We can implement this problem in the fall (it is doable)?

To solve the PBL problem, students were active learners and problem designers, while I was a guide and facilitator of their learning. On Friday, students submitted nine design products that would serve as a plan for their PBL units, which they were expected to implement in the fall. Figure 6.6 (see p. 96) lists the design products. Between the end of the workshop and the beginning of the school year, students fleshed out the design products

Figure 6.3
HOOK FOR "BLOWIN' IN THE WIND" PROBLEM

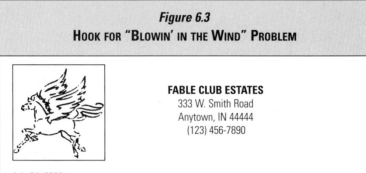

FABLE CLUB ESTATES
333 W. Smith Road
Anytown, IN 44444
(123) 456-7890

July 24, 2000

Residents—

Some of you are meeting on Monday to discuss safety in our community. As you know, because most homes in our community have been installed within the past two years, they meet the HUD standards. Site-built homes do not have to meet such standards. In addition, because mobile homes are built indoors they tend to have better construction.

We anchor all homes at Fable Club as we did in our original Rock Glen Estates property on Smith Road—with four tie-downs on both sides. John Edwards at Rock Glen has used a reliable installer from Fernville for the past 15 years (they're on vacation for two weeks), and we know the installer does a great job. We also think that the great residents we have work hard to maintain their homes and make sure anchoring is appropriate. In the end, proper anchoring according to your manufacturer's specifications is the owner's responsibility. Because proper anchoring virtually ensures the safety of your home in any weather, we feel there is no need for concern at this time. We would like to use the available land at Fable Club to create as many large lots as possible rather than to build a shelter. Shelters are expensive and would no doubt mean a monthly fee increase from our current $245.

We are also concerned about vagrants should the shelter be kept open at all times. Almost no one uses the shelter at Rock Glen, and we've never had any serious damage during storms there. As you know, we're more likely to have damage from poorly constructed storage sheds—or even cars—blowing around than from secured mobile homes. As a resident myself, I feel safe in my home during storms and tornadoes.

A tornado has not struck Anytown for a long time. We think if we were a rural community south of the city, such as Bradley—which was hit last month—we might need to be more concerned about such an occurrence, but our location protects us.

Of course, I'll be glad to listen to any concerns you have and see what we might come up with. I can't be there in the morning, but I do plan to come in around 2:00 p.m. to hear what you have to say. Thank you for your interest. It's another indication of what a great, caring community we have here at Fable Club.

Ronn Quinn
Assistant Park Manager

into a PBL unit. I offered an optional Saturday session in September for this work. After they implemented the units, they wrote a final reflection paper in which they examined issues related to their design, their experience as learners, and their experience as

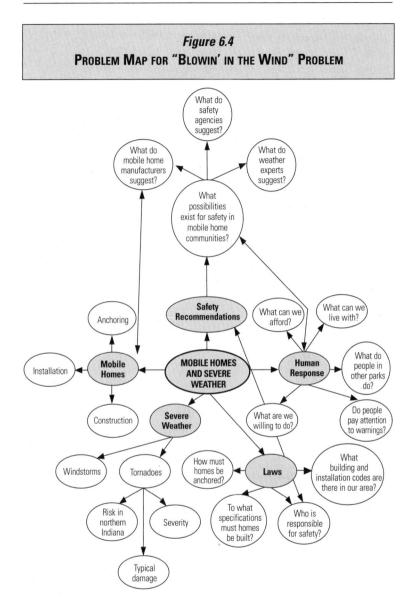

Figure 6.4
PROBLEM MAP FOR "BLOWIN' IN THE WIND" PROBLEM

PBL coaches. Coaching in PBL refers to the teacher's role as a guide for students while they problem-solve (Torp & Sage, 1998).

Instructor's Role

Throughout the week, I used problem-solving strategies to help class members clarify what their students know and need to

Figure 6.5
Rubric for Assessing an Oral Presentation in "Blowin' in the Wind" Problem

Level of Work	Public Speaking	Evidence for Solution	Accuracy of Solution	Fit of Solution to Problem Statement	Group Participation	Quality of Presentation Materials	Interpersonal Communication
			Area to Be Evaluated				
4	Presenters were easy to hear, made appropriate eye contact, and used outstanding vocabulary. Extensive preparation was evident.	Each claim was substantiated by data. Presenters could identify all sources of information.	All data were accurate according to reliable sources.	Solution fits with task and conditions identified in the problem statement.	All group members participated in the presentation.	All materials were appropriate and readable.	All communication was clear, polite, and appropriate.
3	Presenters were mostly easy to hear, made some eye contact, and used adequate vocabulary. Some preparation was evident.	Most claims were substantiated by data. Presenters could identify some sources of information.	Most data were accurate according to reliable sources.	Solution fits with some parts of the problem statement.	All group members participated in the presentation, but some much more than others.	Some materials were appropriate and readable.	Some communication was clear and appropriate.

(continued)

Figure 6.5
—continued—

	Presentation	Claims	Data	Solution	Group Members	Materials	Communication
2	Presenters were difficult to hear, made little eye contact, and used below-average vocabulary. Little preparation was evident.	Some claims were substantiated by data. Presenters had trouble identifying sources of information.	Some data were accurate, or some sources were unreliable.	Solution does not fit with most parts of the problem statement.	One or two group members dominated the presentation.	Materials were inappropriate or unreadable.	Communication was limited or unclear.
1	Presenters were mostly inaudible, made little or no eye contact, and used poor vocabulary. No preparation was evident.	Few or no claims were substantiated by data. Presenters could not identify sources of information.	Little accurate data were presented, or sources were unreliable, or no sources were provided.	Solution does not consider the problem statement at all.	Contribution of some group members was not evident in the presentation.	No materials were used.	Communication was inappropriate, or attempts to communicate did not occur.

Figure 6.6
DESIGN PRODUCTS FOR A PBL UNIT

Design Product	Description
Learner Characteristics	List significant developmental, cognitive, and social-emotional characteristics as well as interests and prior knowledge of the learners you are designing this problem for.
Curriculum Outcomes	List specific curriculum outcomes your students will achieve through this PBL unit.
Problem Map	Construct a focused problem map or web that represents the terrain of the problem your students will meet.
Role and Situation	Indicate clearly the role students will take and the situation they will find themselves in when they meet the problem for the first time.
Hook	Provide documents or materials that will hook students, showing them the relevance of the problem, and introduce them to their role and situation. If the hook includes other elements, such as a person, videotape, or role play, describe each clearly.
Anticipated Problem Statement	Write the anticipated problem statement that you think students will create. Include both the primary *task* or *issue* that students must confront ("How can we . . .") and the *conditions* that must be considered to achieve a satisfactory resolution to the problem ("in such a way that . . .").
Performance Assessment	Specify the final authentic performance assessment in which students will demonstrate what they know and can do (e.g., as legislators, students might present a committee hearing or a committee report). Sketch out a beginning rubric for assessing students' final performance.
Problem Plan	Outline your preliminary teaching and learning plan for your PBL unit. Include the time you expect to spend on the major components, such as teaching and learning events, needed materials and resources, and embedded assessments.
Problem Resources	List preliminary resources you have used in designing the problem and that you expect students will use in their inquiry (e.g., books, articles, Web sites, videotapes, people, and agencies).

know, develop their problems, and examine the fit of their solutions (their PBL units) to their problem statements (what they want the problem to help their students accomplish). This process not only identified big ideas in teaching—such as student motivation, integrative curriculum, teaching style, and philosophy—but also structured the course curriculum and instruction around these big ideas (Brooks & Brooks, 1999). In addition, modeling the PBL process all week helped class members learn what to do when they implemented their own units.

Students sometimes became frustrated with my role as guide, even though I was more directive than I would be with more experienced PBL teachers. They wanted me to give them a good idea for their problem and tell them how they should develop it. I couldn't coach each student simultaneously, even though several were extremely frustrated and needed help. Most realized, at some point during the week, that I was modeling PBL coaching—doing what they would be doing when they implemented their PBL units with their own students.

One positive thing that began to happen was that students started talking to each other about their jobs and the design products they were attempting to develop. They began to coach each other. Their comments on the final university course evaluation reflected how much they valued this coaching experience:

> I was delighted by the brightness, wit, level of commitment displayed (by other teachers), and willingness to help and discuss problems.

> I saw people in our class being open and willing to take chances to encourage learning. I enjoyed this learning experience and the sharing of thoughts with my classmates.

I spent a considerable amount of time and resources planning the course. Preparation was intensive, both to design a PBL experience for the first day that would be a model, and to plan the rest of the week, providing resources to help students design their own problems. I was concerned about the lack of skills these teachers had in locating their own resources. Even though I had suggested to them in a letter before the first day of the course that they bring resources to use in their design products—such as their textbooks or units they had already developed—many did not follow through.

Technology skills and access were also problematic. A number of students were not proficient enough to use the Internet as a resource, and we could not have regular access to the computer lab in the building.

It would not be realistic for me to spend this much time planning all the courses I teach. I did find, however, that the second time through was less demanding, although I remain committed to designing a new problem for the first day each year to ensure I am modeling the use of current and timely issues.

Assessment

I assessed three types of student products: five daily reflection journals, worth five points each; PBL design products submitted on Friday, worth 50 points; and a final reflection paper submitted during the fall semester after students had implemented their units, worth 25 points. I developed the prompts for the journals (Figure 6.7), criteria to assess the design products (Figure 6.8 on p. 100), and guidelines for the final reflection paper (Figure 6.9 on p. 101).

I made it clear that I would grade their design products as first drafts. The tension, however, of trying to understand PBL and submit design products for a grade in one week was difficult for students. Ideally, assessing design products would simply be formative feedback rather than a grade. I did give class members substantive feedback on their design products so that they could make some adjustments before implementing their work as a PBL unit in the fall.

I set the course up as a deferred-grade arrangement because I wanted to encourage students to actually use their PBL units. For any number of reasons, however, some class members were not able to implement their units as planned, so I provided guidelines in the syllabus for writing the final paper for both instances. I also appreciated the opportunity to close the loop as an instructor—to get feedback on what and how teachers learned after actually using PBL in their classrooms, or what they thought about PBL several months after the course. I used responses in the final re-

	Figure 6.7 **PROMPTS FOR DAILY REFLECTION JOURNALS**
Monday	What was the problem-based learning experience like for me as a learner today? What might I take with me from this experience that will help me think what a PBL experience might be like for my own students?
Tuesday	What personal learning issues am I grappling with as I begin to design a PBL unit?
Wednesday	What did I learn from interacting with experienced PBL teachers? What concerns are uppermost for me right now?
Thursday	What are my thoughts on the role of the teacher in PBL? What issues will I find most rewarding or most difficult in my own classroom with this coaching style of teaching?
Friday	What did I learn about myself as a learner and as a teacher this week?

flection papers to examine what effect, if any, this course may have had on their teaching practice.

Outcomes

I focus first on learning outcomes for the students taking the course, then on outcomes related to the format of the course.

Student Learning Outcomes

Each student submitted PBL design products on the last day of the course, and a majority of these products met the criteria I had established (shown in Figure 6.8). Several class members struggled with finding an ill-structured problem rather than simply a student project. From my experience working with teachers new to PBL, the concept of ill-structuredness is the most difficult to grasp and incorporate in problem design. Here are examples of student's PBL design products:

• A kindergarten teacher designed a problem around students' losing personal items and the current lost-and-found policy in their school.
• A 5th grade teacher designed her problem around the real issue of whether or not Puerto Rico should become a state.

Figure 6.8
CRITERIA FOR EVALUATING DESIGN PRODUCTS

Area to Be Evaluated	Criteria
Selection and development of problem topic	Problem map is coherent and complete; some problem resource selection is evident.
Appropriateness of problem to target audience and subject areas	Problem issue fits curriculum; problem is developmentally appropriate for grade level.
Alignment of unit with principles of PBL	Problem is ill-structured and shows collaborative inquiry; assessments are authentic.
Accuracy of design products	Spelling is correct, and information is accurate.
Completeness of unit	All design products are complete.

Students acted as advisors on Indiana's position to a local congressperson's office.

• A middle school teacher placed her students in the role of consultants who must determine a course of action for rising adolescent tobacco use in the student population at her school.

• A middle school French teacher in a school with a French immersion program designed her problem so that students would create a marketing plan (in French) for the school store.

• An adult education teacher invited her students to determine whether or not an outdoor smoking shelter should be built on the adult education campus.

• A counseling student experimented with using a PBL approach in her work with families of developmentally delayed preschool children.

Class members summarized their experiences in the week-long course in a final journal prompt: What did I learn about myself as a learner and as a teacher this week? Here are several responses:

> I relearned everything about being a student—the panic, the frustration, the great moment of inspiration, the fun of learning, the joy of working with delightful people.

> I am used to taking a problem and running with it. Group work (the first day's tornado unit) forced me to slow down, listen to others' opinions, and process information cooperatively.

Figure 6.9
GUIDELINES FOR THE FINAL REFLECTION PAPER

Guiding Questions

What did I learn about myself as a teacher from this PBL experience?

What was hardest for me about my role as a PBL coach as I implemented the problem?

What did I learn about my students from this PBL experience?

What surprised me most about my students' work in the problem?

What did I learn (or remember) about curriculum, instruction, and assessment?

How did other people (parents, other teachers, and administrators) react to PBL?

What did I learn about the design of my PBL unit? What would I change if I were to do this problem again?

What did I learn about using learning resources for student inquiry in PBL? What resources were hardest to locate, and how can I facilitate acquiring resources in the future?

What will I carry with me in my teaching from this experience?

What is one burning question I still have about PBL? (The instructor will respond in writing.)

Assessment Criteria

Answers each prompt completely.

Demonstrates higher-order thinking related to using PBL in the classroom.

Gives specific information about what worked well, what didn't, and why.

Shows thoughtfulness related to own teaching and includes feedback that can be used in the future.

Demonstrates a developing understanding of the PBL process and of teaching and learning in general.

Optional: You may attach student work samples or a videotape (no more than three).

I realized that this type of active thinking is productive but very draining. It reminds me of labor—in a good way. I really got a lot more out of this class than in other homework-lecture courses.

I learned that the time well spent in planning really does reap benefits. With PBL, there really is no way to avoid planning. . . . Once I am prepared, the rest should flow.

I learned a great deal about what I value in myself and in the working relationships I develop with families.

On both the first and last days of the course, I asked students to write definitions of effective teaching. It was clear that they brought a broad spectrum of teaching approaches to the class. Their beginning definitions, primarily focusing on technical teaching skills, ranged from student centered and communication oriented, to interactive and individualized, to behavioral. Although five days is a short time, their conceptions of effective teaching on Friday differed noticeably from Monday's definitions. Most students were now using terms like "guide/facilitate/coach student learning"— terminology much more representative of a constructivist view of the teacher's role. "Critical thinking" was another phrase mentioned repeatedly. On the first day, few students mentioned assessment; on the last day, a number of students said that teachers should use authentic assessments to guide student learning.

I used students' final reflection papers, submitted in the fall, to get a glimpse of what they were actually applying in new understandings about teaching. In general, regardless of initial teaching philosophies, these educators made changes in the way they viewed themselves and their work with learners (Torp & Sage, 1998; Sage & Torp, 1997). They asked questions about problems and curriculum that had not occurred to them earlier. They shifted to a more facilitative role as educators, rather than "controllers" or "tellers." One interesting outcome was that, as they trusted their learners more, they realized the learners had what they needed inside themselves to learn. All teachers found that their PBL units went in directions they didn't exactly expect, but they were pleased with the results. Finally, they reported changes in how they viewed problems and problem solving. They were more thoughtful and thorough in addressing their real-life problem situations.

Class Format Outcomes

Class members consistently reported that a real experience with PBL as a learner on the first day helped them move to a deeper, more personal understanding of the strategy. Here is one student's comment:

> The PBL experience today, for me, was the answer to most of my questions about PBL. When I signed up for this class, I had no idea what it was. After reading the assignment, I had an intellectual idea of what it was. Now I have a working, real understanding of what it is. There is no better way to learn than through real-life experience. Now I have a model to use to create a similar experience for my students.

Another helpful portion of the class, according to student journals and university course evaluations, was the interaction with experienced PBL teachers on Wednesday morning. I invited teachers I had worked with to conduct minisessions in several breakout rooms, describing PBL units they had designed and implemented. Here are student comments about this activity:

> The PBL teachers are very excited about this strategy for teaching and learning. I was impressed by their excitement and creativity! . . . I also learned that I should not just give up if my first PBL unit is not as successful as I would like it to be.

> It helped clear some of the fuzzy parts like, where do I get a problem? They just seemed to pull one from everyday local concerns. . . . It was great to see the teachers so excited about PBL. Sometimes I think teachers forget that learning should be fun!

The minisessions seemed particularly helpful because they came immediately after a challenging day in which students had struggled to select and develop ideas for PBL units of their own. If I had lacked access to experienced PBL teachers, I would have provided additional examples of successful PBL units through articles and videotapes.

Problems

One of the biggest issues in this course, and in other teacher workshops I have led, was to deal with the confusion, frustration, and fear teachers can feel when they struggle with fitting PBL into both their curricula and their personal understanding of teaching. I often use the analogy of marathon runners "hitting the wall" at a certain point in the race. The students and I encountered the wall

Tuesday and Wednesday as they struggled with generating ideas for PBL units, and I struggled with my role as coach to mentor and support them without jumping in to solve their problems.

Designing problems is not a linear process, but rather a creative one that sometimes moves in fits and starts. Design work cannot start only with curriculum outcomes or only with a problem idea, but must consider both simultaneously. Many students were overwhelmed with this process, at least for part of the course. It is difficult to have only a few days to complete this work and then to have it graded at the end. Given the diversity of students taking this course, working on one consistent problem that fit all their teaching situations would have been impossible.

Another problem was that not all students were taking the course because they wanted to explore and use PBL; many were simply looking for a one-week summer course they could take for needed credits in their programs. The course did not fit what many students had become accustomed to expecting in graduate courses. They had to take a much more active role as learners and work much harder than in some other courses. For some students, designing a problem for a grade was a difficult class exercise rather than the "transforming experience" I had hoped it would be. Even in these cases, however, I was surprised by the thoughtfulness of students' reflections each day; they were almost forced to consider their philosophy of teaching by the nature of the course.

The biggest problem I faced, which I have not fully resolved, was how to help such a variety of educators find ways to make PBL meaningful in their work. As a professor new to this campus, I made the assumption I was going to be working with all classroom teachers in a summer workshop. Therefore, I designed the course to be most relevant for K–12 classroom teachers. The way I had set up the curriculum did not make sense to the counseling students or the speech therapist in their work. They couldn't necessarily design a PBL unit in the same way a classroom teacher would. They ended up focusing more on the process of PBL in their work, which one reported was extremely valuable, but I was still dissatisfied with the fit of this course for their work.

Suggestions and Conclusions

Overall, I consider this course a success, both in terms of student learning outcomes and in student satisfaction with the course. Here are several suggestions I have taken to heart and would recommend to other teacher educators:

• Be sure that students encounter PBL throughout the course in the form of experiencing PBL as learners, using the PBL process to design their own units, talking with experienced PBL teachers, and seeing as many examples of PBL as possible. The entire course should be PBL.

• Consider the time frame of such a course carefully. The one-week intensive format works well for an immersion in PBL and for students to quickly develop a sense of community, but it may simply not include enough thinking and work time for some students. If you choose a one-week format, you will need students to do some reading and thinking before the course starts. They should come prepared with ideas and resources for PBL units.

• Provide numerous opportunities for students to consider their own philosophies of teaching and learning. Many teachers had never examined their educational beliefs and reported great benefit from talking and writing about their philosophies. This awareness is critical for teachers encountering PBL for the first time.

• Create a warm, supportive classroom climate to offset the tremendous cognitive and emotional challenge such a course can be for many students. I sent students a letter about the course before it began, which included preparation suggestions; chose a room with tables where students could work comfortably and get to know each other; provided a simple breakfast the first day; spent a good deal of time on introductions; allowed a generous lunch break each day; and allowed maximum flexibility on where and how students did their individual design work. The instructor should also budget time to discuss difficult teaching issues.

• Keep the class size as small as possible, around 10–15 students. One way to offset a large class is to encourage students who are practicing teachers to sign up in pairs or small groups, so that several people can work together on a grade level or interdisciplinary problem. Another idea is to invite experienced PBL teachers to help as design mentors. I plan to include selected students from this class as mentors for future classes.

• Provide options (and examples) for students to design PBL experiences for many different educational settings. My class members' students or clients ranged from preschoolers to the elderly. An academically oriented PBL unit is not the most appropriate product for all persons who take the course (e.g., principals, counselors, and therapists). The instructor needs to offer alternative assessments, such as a description of how these students might apply the PBL process in their work, and provide examples of how others have developed PBL units in these areas. For example, the principal in my course designed an experience around the real problem of developing a long-range technology plan for her building. Subjects like art, music, or foreign language often involve problems and performances as part of their content. PBL can be a natural fit, but students may need examples to understand the fit.

* * *

In conclusion, I have described a one-week, summer graduate course designed for inservice professionals to help them develop PBL units for their own settings. Students experienced PBL as learners, designed their own PBL units, and practiced coaching skills. Most then implemented their units in their own teaching situations. Planning and implementing the entire course from a constructivist, problem-based perspective were important but also challenging for the learners and me. Students reported increased enthusiasm for their teaching, a change in their teaching practices, and a difficult but stimulating learning experience.

Using PBL to teach PBL was an effective strategy. By placing ourselves with our students in the midst of an authentic and complex problem, we can become a collaborative community of learners. Walking the talk together will help us meet the challenges of moving forward in education in the new millennium.

REFERENCES

Brooks, M. G., & Brooks, J. G. (1999). *In search of understanding: The case for constructivist classrooms* (2nd ed.). Alexandria, VA: Association for Supervision and Curriculum Development.

A popular book outlining the basis for creating classrooms using constructivist theories of learning.

Delisle, R. (1997). *How to use problem-based learning in the classroom.* Alexandria, VA: Association for Supervision and Curriculum Development.

A practical book detailing how to undertake PBL. It provides examples of PBL units that can be used in K–12 settings.

Fosnot, C. T. (1989). *Enquiring teachers, enquiring learners: A constructivist approach for teaching.* New York: Teachers College Press.

A book outlining an innovative model of teacher education. It is based on constructivist philosophy, which engages teachers as learners and investigators.

Interstate New Teacher Assessment and Support Consortium (INTASC). (1992). *Model standards for beginning teacher licensing and development: A resource for state dialogue.* Washington, DC: Council for Chief State School Officers.

A report outlining 10 standards for effective teaching that many states are basing new teacher licensure standards on.

Richardson, V. (Ed.) (1997). *Constructivist teacher education: Building new understandings.* London: Falmer Press.

A book presenting a number of views. It describes several courses in which teacher educators put constructivist learning theories into teaching practice.

Sage, S. M., & Torp, L. T. (1997). What does it take to become a teacher of problem-based learning? *Journal of Staff Development, 18*(4), 32–36.

An article detailing a PBL professional development program for inservice teachers. It presents lessons learned about teaching teachers how to use PBL.

Torp, L., & Sage, S. (1998). *Problems as possibilities: Problem-based learning for K–12 education.* Alexandria, VA: Association for Supervision and Curriculum Development.

A foundational book providing reasons that PBL works with students, a process for designing and implementing problems, and several examples of PBL in K–12 settings.

7 Classroom Action Research as Problem-Based Learning

Gwynn Mettetal

MOST TEACHERS TAKE GRADUATE COURSES TO MAINTAIN THEIR LICENS-ing, and they participate in staff development to improve their teaching. Such professional development often takes the form of workshops on various topics, usually offered during teacher in-service days or after school. Teachers often complain that these workshops are irrelevant, one-shot efforts and that they rarely lead to actual changes in the classroom. In two school districts in northern Indiana, we have been using classroom action research in staff development to counter the charge of irrelevance. The program's design mirrors PBL in many ways, and we find that it has the same advantages as PBL in developing skills and motivation.

Classroom action research (CAR) is the systematic investigation of what works in the classroom, with the goal of improving student learning. Although we know a great deal about good teaching in general, every teaching situation is unique in many areas, such as content, level, student skills and learning styles, and teacher skills and teaching styles. Teachers conducting classroom action research ask what works best in a particular teaching situation. These teacher-researchers typically gather both quantitative and qualitative data from several sources and share their results with those directly affected, so that others may take action based on the findings.

Teachers conducting CAR follow the same general steps common to any research study: carefully formulate a question; seek information (qualitative and quantitative); analyze data to answer the question; draw conclusions from analyses; and take action based on the conclusions. In contrast to traditional, formal educational research, a practitioner rather than a professor usually conducts CAR. CAR achieves validity by comparing several types of data rather than trying experimental designs. Results from CAR may not generalize to other situations; rather, they help the researcher make good decisions about the researcher's own situation. Obviously, CAR is less complex and more immediately applicable than a large university study.

As Figure 7.1 shows, classroom action research follows the PBL process closely, with a few notable exceptions. In PBL, course teachers construct a real-life problem and present it to students in a realistic manner. In CAR, teacher-researchers decide what problem to work on, drawing from their classrooms and school context. Thus, the CAR problem is not *like* real life; it *is* real life. In both PBL and CAR, the problem is ill-structured, can be answered

Figure 7.1
COMPARISON OF PROBLEM-BASED LEARNING AND CLASSROOM ACTION RESEARCH

Area	Problem-Based Learning	Classroom Action Research
Source for Problem	*Course teacher.*	*Teacher-researcher.*
Motivation	*Solving a lifelike problem.*	*Solving a real-life problem.*
Type of Problem	Ill-structured; without one right answer; changes as it unfolds.	Ill-structured; without one right answer; changes as it unfolds.
Problem Statement	*Defined after identifying what's needed.*	*Refined from original vague statement.*
Information Sources	Library, Internet, and experts.	Library, Internet, experts, and original data the teacher-researcher has collected.
Role of Teacher	Facilitator and coach.	Facilitator, coach, and researcher.
Assessment	Presentation to an authentic audience.	Presentation to an authentic audience, but work is primarily self-assessed.

Note: Primary differences are italicized.

in more than one way, and may change as it unfolds. In PBL, students define a problem statement after they have identified what they know and what they need to know. In CAR, teacher-researchers refine their question from something vague (e.g., How can we help Hispanic students make the transition to high school?) to a question that can be answered more clearly (e.g., Will a weekend camp experience make Hispanic students feel more positive about school?).

In both PBL and CAR, participants work in teams to gather information from a variety of sources. PBL participants use this information to generate solutions to their problem. CAR participants not only use information to refine their problem, but also gather original data, such as student test scores and attitude measures, to determine the best solution for their problem.

In both PBL and CAR, the teacher is a facilitator and a coach. The CAR teacher must also be a researcher to help participants gather and interpret original data.

Problem solutions may be presented in various ways. In PBL, solutions are presented in an authentic manner to an authentic audience (if possible). In CAR, the authentic audience is the teacher-researcher who has the actual problem. School districts that I work with also ask each research team to present their findings at a research fair, which is attended by teachers, school administrators, and school board members. Teams may also present findings to a parent-teacher organization, school board, and other groups.

Context for PBL/CAR

I work with two local K–12 school districts on staff development plans that encourage teams of teachers to plan and complete action research projects. Teachers are invited by the school district's office of curriculum and instruction to form small teams to work on a common problem. Although most teams are from the same school, some contain members from other schools. Participants range from first-year teachers to building principals. Most have little or no training in research methods. Teams work throughout the school year on their projects and present their findings during a spring research fair. Their participation is structured as a PBL project: They choose a problem—which an advisory board of teachers, administrators, university faculty, and parents approves—then they gather information to solve the problem. Staff developers, mentors, and consultants provide support as needed. Each year, 60 to 70 teachers participate in each district.

Purposes for Using PBL/CAR

The two primary goals of these districtwide PBL/CAR initiatives are to help teachers learn the process of inquiry and to improve student learning by discovering what works best in the classroom. These goals differ from those of traditional staff development goals in two important ways. First, no particular teaching model or strategy is presented to teachers. Rather, the focus is on solving problems the teachers themselves pose through classroom action research. Second, the teachers need to find their own answers, rather than rely on "experts" from the main office or the university to tell them what works best in their individual situations.

Details of the PBL/CAR Assignment

The PBL/CAR districtwide project has a clear process, and Figure 7.2 (see p. 112) shows an overview of that process.

Teachers sign up for the projects in teams of two to four and arrive at our first meeting in the early fall with a general problem topic in mind. One district give broad topic areas; the other allows any topic. One of the first tasks they are given is to turn their general topic into a research question. In some other models of PBL and CAR, teachers are given their question or problem. We believe that allowing teachers to choose their own topic is much more motivating and useful to them. Nevertheless, we do guide teams in developing a question that is relevant, feasible, and focused on student learning. For example, one team arrived with the general

---

Figure 7.2
OVERVIEW OF THE PBL/CAR PROCESS

1. In the summer, the school district staff writes a grant proposal for Educate Indiana funds. I help with the section on the districtwide PBL/CAR project. This funding will provide stipends and materials for the teacher-researchers.

2. In early October, teachers are invited to form teams and submit a brief proposal consisting of their research question (the problem) and some ideas of how they will answer that question. An advisory board reviews these proposals and assigns mentors to each team.

3. In November, I lead a workshop that helps teams and their mentors refine their research question/problem and choose appropriate research strategies.

4. In early December, revised proposals are sent to the advisory board for review.

5. Teams begin work on their PBL/CAR problem.

6. In mid-February, teams and mentors meet to discuss their progress. The advisory board reviews brief progress reports. When a team is having difficulty, the board arranges for assistance, such as resources or consultants.

7. In late April, teams submit to the advisory board for approval a final report describing their question/problem, research strategies, and their findings/solution.

8. In early May, teams present their work at the action research fair and banquet. School board members, advisory board members, and the public are invited.

9. In the following months, teams present their work to other authentic audiences.

---

topic of multiple intelligences. Their refined question was, "How can we use multiple-intelligences theory to improve learning in our classroom?" This question would also be a good PBL question.

Each research team turns in a proposal that includes the team's research question and research strategy. An advisory board approves these proposals, suggesting refinements and changes as needed.

Resources

We provide participants with information about the inquiry process through workshops on research design, literature searches, and data collection and analysis. Each team also has a mentor who is an experienced researcher, and books on classroom research methods are available for team use (see Additional Resources at the end of the chapter). Teams develop research skills to find published information about their problem topic and to generate their own information by collecting quantitative and qualitative data from their classes.

Project Requirements

Teams are required to turn in a proposal for their project that includes their refined question and plans for answering the question. Figure 7.3 (see p. 114) describes one district's guidelines for the projects.

At midyear, teams turn in brief progress reports. Both the proposals and reports are evaluated by an advisory board that includes teacher-mentors, a parent, several school administrators, several community members, and me. We give teams feedback to improve their plans.

At the end of the year, teams report their findings in two ways. First, they complete an abstract and a 5- to 20-page written report that includes their problem, research methods, and findings. Figure 7.4 (see p. 115) shows an example of an abstract. Second, they present their problem at a research fair, which is modeled on school science fairs. Teams use posters, videotapes, artifacts, and other materials to explain their problem to others.

We assess individual accountability by asking teams to submit a written plan of their individual contributions at the beginning of the process and then to describe what they actually did at the end. Some project participants may also choose to enroll in an action research independent study course for university credit.

Instructor's Role

I have collaborated on these projects with two school districts, one for three and one for five years. The exact process changes slightly from year to year, but common needs exist. I work closely with the school district's director of curriculum and instruction as each school district grant for the CAR program is written. (These are Educate Indiana grants to the school district through the Indiana Department of Education.) The grants detail the types of

---

Figure 7.3
GUIDELINES FOR PBL/CAR PROJECT PROPOSALS

Proposal must be a team effort (two to four people).

Proposal must focus on strategies that improve student learning, especially those issues that relate to the identified problems, issues, and needs (i.e., poor test results, reading and math skill development, development of strategies to assist students affected by poverty and mobility, graduation-related needs, transitioning issues that affect student success, and the disparity in academic achievement and retention for our Hispanic population).

Literature review must include research on learning and the inquiry-reflection processes and research on your studied strategy or (if none available) on similar strategies.

Proposal must include strategies for teaching students how to reflect on their own work so they can begin to develop an understanding of how they learn.

Teams must share the process of action research (inquiry-reflection) they are using with their students.

Proposal must have the endorsement of the building principal. Preference will be given to proposals that address issues that are part of a school's improvement plan.

Building principals and the advisory board must guide teachers in collecting parental consent and other ethical issues when appropriate.

Source: Elkhart Community Schools, Elkhart, Indiana.

---

problems that will be explored and the outcomes that are expected. These funds are used primarily for small stipends for researchers, mentors, workshops, and research materials.

I teach workshops on strategies of inquiry and help teams as needed. As a member of the advisory board, I evaluate and give feedback on proposals, strategies, and midyear and final reports, making myself available by telephone and e-mail to answer questions from teams or their mentors. Other activities include attending the research fair to question teams about their findings and teaching the course for those who enroll for university credit.

Assessment

Because PBL/CAR projects are staff development opportunities and not a university course, no grades are assigned. Teams who do not meet minimum standards, however, do not receive their stipends for participation. Here are the minimum standards for successful projects:

Figure 7.4
EXAMPLE OF ONE TEAM'S FINAL ABSTRACT

Research Topic: Peer Mediation

Questions Researched
Do students sense enough conflict in the student body to make a mediation program worthwhile to pursue?

Is the peer mediation process/program at North Side Middle School producing a positive influence on school climate?

Do students accept the peer mediation program as an effective/useful tool in solving conflict?

Is the mediation process, and are the mentors, promoting an environment that will help students solve conflict and learn skills that will carry over into helping students solve conflict that is not formally mediated?

Is the school staff supporting the mediation program by making positive reference to the program and making appropriate referrals?

Methods Used to Research
Pre- and postquestionnaires for students to give their input.

Interviews with staff members, interviews with selected students, and interviews with peer mediators.

Study of completed mediations to determine (1) success rate as viewed by the mediators; (2) thoughtfulness of the proposed solution to the conflict; and (3) statistics regarding referrals. Who makes them? What were the issues? What were the problems? Evaluation and comparison of all data.

Findings of Effects on Students
1. As the year progressed, an increasing number of students were aware of student conflict at North Side Middle School.

2. As the year progressed, an increasing number of students became familiar with the peer mediation program.

3. Girls generally viewed peer mediation as a more useful/effective tool than did boys.

4. At this time near the end of the school year, nearly one half of the student body believes that peer mediation has helped some students solve conflict.

5. More than one half of the students at North Side "hope" that peer mediation will be available at the high school that they attend.

Source: North Side Middle School, Elkhart, Indiana.

• An abstract following a specified format (shown in Figure 7.4).

• A longer, more detailed final report describing the problem, what the team has done to investigate it, findings, and conclusions. Papers should have at least five outside references. Figure 7.5 (see p. 116) shows criteria for the final report.

• Presentation at the research fair.

• Presentation to at least two other authentic audiences, such as the school parent-teacher organization or a staff meeting.

Teachers who enroll for course credit are graded by usual graduate-level standards. I use a mastery learning model: Students may revise and resubmit their final report until it reaches A quality.

During the proposal review, the advisory board approves team problem statements, so attention at this final point is focused on data collection, data analysis, and conclusions drawn. The advisory board assesses midyear and final team reports. When reports are insufficient, the board returns them to teams for revision. Returns rarely happen, though, because both the advisory board and mentors review each team's work frequently during the year.

Outcomes

Using PBL/CAR in this staff development initiative is extremely successful. Participants become more skilled and confident in using inquiry (problem-solving) methods, one of our

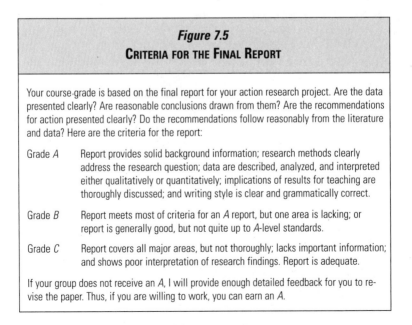

Figure 7.5
CRITERIA FOR THE FINAL REPORT

Your course-grade is based on the final report for your action research project. Are the data presented clearly? Are reasonable conclusions drawn from them? Are the recommendations for action presented clearly? Do the recommendations follow reasonably from the literature and data? Here are the criteria for the report:

Grade A   Report provides solid background information; research methods clearly address the research question; data are described, analyzed, and interpreted either qualitatively or quantitatively; implications of results for teaching are thoroughly discussed; and writing style is clear and grammatically correct.

Grade B   Report meets most of criteria for an A report, but one area is lacking; or report is generally good, but not quite up to A-level standards.

Grade C   Report covers all major areas, but not thoroughly; lacks important information; and shows poor interpretation of research findings. Report is adequate.

If your group does not receive an A, I will provide enough detailed feedback for you to revise the paper. Thus, if you are willing to work, you can earn an A.

primary goals. On a survey after the research fair, one teacher-researcher wrote, "[CAR] helps all teachers to improve their critical-thinking skills and expand their perspective on issues." We find that students need less formal instruction in inquiry methods each year because as new teachers join the program, there are plenty of project veterans to explain the basic process to them. We also notice that many of these veteran researchers are becoming interested in more complex problems; thus, the mentors and I still provide much information on research design and data analysis. One survey response said, "This year's research was much more focused than last year's. We learned how to attack the problem."

PBL/CAR also meets our second main goal, to improve student learning, by finding out what works in a particular classroom. One teacher wrote, "Using my own school children in the study shows me what works best." By becoming actively involved in gathering and interpreting information, teachers are able to determine which teaching strategies (or aspects of teaching strategies) are most effective in their classroom setting. Most participants change teaching strategies as the result of their findings.

We find that this process has two other desirable outcomes. Teachers report that participation makes them feel more professional because they can now answer parent questions about teaching strategies by saying that they have investigated this problem themselves and then explaining their findings. Teachers also report an increase in collegiality from their work with team members at their sites. One teacher wrote, "The professional growth comes from within—constructing our own learning instead of someone teaching us."

Problems

We encountered several problems during the first years of this PBL/CAR initiative. We found that team size was critical. Teams larger than four had trouble getting together, and some members' participation became marginalized. A "team" of one person was much more likely to feel overwhelmed. This variety in team size occurred because we originally asked teachers to form their own teams based on their interest in a particular problem. To maximize the benefits of the PBL/CAR process for all, we now require that teams have two to four educators.

Another problem was finding enough mentors for teams. In the early years, I used public school administrators and local college professors. When the second school district began its program, it recruited experienced teacher-researchers from the first school district. By the second year in each district, most mentors came from each district's own pool of experienced teacher-researchers.

Incentives for teacher participation are a potential problem. These projects require a large investment of time and effort from teacher-researchers and mentors. One school district allows each teacher-researcher to take two days' leave from the classroom and pays for substitute teachers. College credit is a valuable incentive for most teachers, but tuition can be expensive. PBL/CAR funding comes through the Indiana State Department of Education, which funds a number of innovative programs each year. Funds might also be sought through federal programs or private granting agencies.

Suggestions and Conclusions

We find that using PBL/CAR is an excellent tool for staff development. Teachers learn to feel comfortable with the process of inquiry, and they discover what works for their own classroom. Follow-up evaluations indicate that project participants are highly motivated and believe that the information they gain is valuable. Most teachers feel that student learning in their classroom improves as the result of their project.

Although traditional PBL begins with a problem designed by the instructor, we find that allowing teams to design their own real-life problem is an important option, with instructors and mentors assisting in refining the problem statement. Practicing teachers are motivated by using actual problems they are facing in the classroom as the focus of their PBL experience. Problem topics may be limited to a particular content area if desired, such as reading or classroom management. We believe, however, that teachers will be optimally motivated by working on real classroom problems. Indeed, if the goal of classroom action research is to help the teacher take informed action, a problem relevant to the particular situation is required.

Administrative support is crucial to the success of the program in both school districts. Local school district administrators write the state grant proposals that provide stipends for teachers and mentors and resources such as books and supplies. Administrators also provide support by encouraging participation from each school in the district.

In conclusion, classroom action research functions as authentic, individualized PBL for educators. Teachers engaged in CAR are motivated to learn content and skills as they solve real problems in the same way as students engaged in PBL. PBL/CAR projects can be used in graduate education courses or as part of school district inservice staff development. In the words of one teacher-researcher when asked what she would tell a colleague who was considering PBL/CAR, "Just do it. It's worth the effort!"

ADDITIONAL RESOURCES

Bell, J. (1993). *Doing your research project: A guide for first-time researchers in education and social science.* (2nd ed.). Philadelphia: Open University Press.

   One of the best "how to" guides for classroom research. It has excellent examples of data collection and analysis techniques and is particularly strong on quantitative methods.

Calhoun, E. (1994). *How to use action research in the self-renewing school.* Alexandria, VA: Association for Supervision and Curriculum Development.

   A book showing how to develop a schoolwide question or problem and then how to work together to solve it.

Hubbard, R. S., & Power, B. (1993). *The art of classroom inquiry: A handbook for teacher-researchers.* Portsmouth, NH: Heinemann.

   Another "how to" book with great examples that are particularly strong on qualitative techniques for conducting classroom action research.

McNiff, J., Lomax, P., & Whitehead, J. (1996). *You and your action research project*. New York: Routledge.

A book guiding the teacher through the reflective process of action research.

Mettetal, G. (n.d.). Gwynn Mettetal, Associate Professor of Educational Psychology, Division of Education, Indiana University South Bend [Web site]. Available: http://www.iusb.edu/~gmetteta (2000, September 21).

The author's Web site providing research on teaching and learning, resources for teacher-researchers, and links to other educational Web sites.

Sagor, R. (1993). *How to conduct collaborative action research*. Alexandria, VA: Association for Supervision and Curriculum Development.

An easy-to-read introduction to the action research process.

8 Frequently Asked Questions About Problem-Based Learning

BARBARA B. LEVIN WITH CAROL D. DEAN AND JEAN W. PIERCE

TO CONCLUDE THIS BOOK, WE OFFER OUR RESPONSES TO SOME FREquently asked questions (FAQs) that students, teachers, teacher educators, and administrators often ask as they learn about PBL. Although our answers are not definitive, we do provide realistic responses based on our experiences using PBL with prospective and experienced teachers. We have also used PBL with K–12 students, so we bring this additional perspective to our answers. If you have further questions or wish to seek additional information, we point you to the References and the Additional Resources sections at the end of each chapter. They list articles and books about PBL, as well as Internet addresses for sites where you can gather information and join discussion groups with teachers currently using PBL.

What makes a good problem?

Good problems have common characteristics and elements, which we highlight here. They have these characteristics:

• Authentic and messy or ill-structured, not readily solved, compelling for learners, focused on real-world situations, and related to curriculum objectives and important content.

• Academically rigorous, offering opportunities for students to practice essential skills, such as conducting research, writing, solving problems, and communicating.
  • Relevant to learners' interests and needs.

Here is what good problems should do:

• Catalyze learners to exercise their creative and critical-thinking skills.
  • Accommodate a variety of teaching and learning styles.
  • Allow learners to make connections to the real world.
  • Contain subproblems to help clarify the main problem.
  • Allow for several hypotheses and problem solutions—rather than one simple or obviously correct answer.
  • Use an inquiry process that encourages learners to conduct research so that they can propose solutions.
  • Provide for problem solutions that are the result of integrating knowledge from several sources and a variety of disciplines.
  • Require the acquisition of new knowledge.
  • Plan for a product of some kind to evaluate learning.

What are the critical elements of the problem-solving framework underlying problem-based learning?

First, a problem should be complex enough to require that learners use a problem-solving process similar to the scientific method of inquiry. PBL works best by using a problem-solving framework that includes

• Interpreting and defining the problem.
  • Generating questions that need to be answered about the problem.
  • Conducting research to find answers to the questions.
  • Proposing a variety of hypotheses and potential problem solutions that are warranted by the data collected.

• Discussing the pros and cons of these potential solutions.

• Selecting and presenting potential problem solutions to a real audience.

Second, PBL should begin with learners determining what they know about the problem from their existing knowledge and experience. Learners might use a simple matrix to answer the following questions: What do we know? What do we need to know? What issues are emerging? What are our hypotheses? Where can we find more information? Examples of how to apply a problem-solving framework to specific problems are found in Chapters 3 and 6.

Third, participants need to learn to work together as a team—to share information with a group, listen to others, provide appropriate feedback, accept feedback, share tasks, achieve consensus on a proposed solution, and defend the solution with logical arguments.

What are the similarities and differences between *problem-based learning* and *project-based learning?*

Projects are often embedded in problem-based learning, especially at the presentation stage, when it is time to recommend potential problem solutions to a real audience. The form that the presentation takes is usually a product or performance, such as a multimedia presentation, a poster, an oral presentation, or a debate. Project-based learning often comes at the end of the problem-based learning process.

Similarities

• Both are learner centered, focused on authentic tasks, and provide opportunities for learners to construct meaning rather than just receive it.

• Learners have opportunities to practice a variety of skills they need for success in school and real life.

• Learners may work collaboratively with partners or in small groups.

• The problem is centered on content to be explored.

• Work can be assessed in a variety of ways.

• Learners plan, solve problems, and make decisions throughout the process.

• The teacher facilitates rather than directs, although in problem-based learning, the teacher may act more as a coach or tutor to scaffold the problem-solving experience with timely questions.

Differences

• PBL focuses on the problem and its solutions; products are a part of the solution. Project-based learning focuses on projects or products.

• PBL requires that learners research and study information to generate several possible solutions to a problem. Project-based learning concentrates on creating a product or project.

• PBL usually involves cooperative group work. In project-based learning, learners are more likely to work autonomously on their projects.

Who uses problem-based learning?

Too often thought of as a learning method for "gifted" students or for those in an "honors program," PBL is for students and teachers of all ages and developmental levels and in all disciplines. PBL is a good method to engage and challenge bright as well as reluctant learners, especially those whose preferred learning style is active and interactive or who have been turned off by more didactic teaching strategies. PBL encourages creativity and higher-order thinking.

PBL mimics real-life learning because the problems are authentic to the field of study and beg to be solved. We think that teachers who use a student-centered, constructivist approach will be comfortable with PBL. Those who prefer more traditional and didactic modes of instruction will probably not be as comfortable with PBL's ill-structured nature initially. But we encourage them to learn about and practice PBL so that they can add it to their repertoire of teaching strategies and use it when needed.

Why use problem-based learning?

Problem-based learning helps engage students in learning, thus shifting the focus from *teaching* to *learning.* Students understand the relevance of what they are learning and take ownership of it. PBL helps educators prepare students for the real-world, messy problems they will face outside school.

Retention and transfer of learning can be improved by using PBL. People do not solve real problems by answering multiple-choice questions, filling in the blanks on worksheets, or even writing five-paragraph essays. Certainly, learning to be a teacher cannot happen without engaging in the real world of classrooms where a multitude of problems must be solved each day. The kinds of problems teachers face require gathering information, evaluating that information, using critical-thinking skills, generating creative solutions, and trying out various solutions to problems. PBL is one way to simulate real-world problem solving, learn important content material, and practice important skills under the leadership of a teacher who acts as a guide, coach, and facilitator of student learning.

What are some good assessment methods?

To evaluate both individual and group work, teachers should use a variety of formative and summative assessments. All assessments should focus on cognitive objectives, content to be learned, and specific process skills. Ongoing assessments may include rubrics, checklists, individual learning logs, and evaluation by outside observers and experts. Observing, questioning, and guiding discussions are opportunities for teachers to assess informally. Final presentations and products are evaluated as group work. Teacher feedback and learners' self-evaluation assess individual work.

How does problem-based learning fit into my school, district, or state curriculum?

The teacher should identify the content and skills to be learned during PBL, aligning them with school, district, state, and national curriculum standards. Problems can and should be written to build a knowledge base consistent with the curriculum guidelines for each school, district, and class. One of PBL's main goals is to help learners acquire new knowledge, but practicing essential skills and developing important attitudes are also important. The teacher should pay explicit attention to identifying cognitive, affective, and social skills that students need to learn and practice. These skills become specific objectives and serve as anchors for decisions about what kinds of PBL activities might be encouraged. PBL should complement and enhance required curriculum content, not conflict with it.

What is the teacher's role?

The teacher takes on many roles during PBL. The main role is to determine and carry out curriculum requirements. Besides selecting the content and skills to focus on, the teacher locates potential resources that students can use to research the problem and construct the problem statement and focus questions, and plans how to introduce the problem so that students are motivated to become involved.

Once the teacher has designed the problem, then her role shifts to that of facilitator, coach, or tutor, to be ready to scaffold learning by asking questions, probing for deeper understanding, and assessing student and group progress. The teacher should be prepared to ask high-level, thought-provoking questions and provide relevant feedback. Teachers help students develop critical-thinking and research skills. The teacher's role includes designing different types of assessments.

What is the student's role?

The student's role is an active one and likely quite different from typical approaches to learning. In PBL, students go for deep and nuanced understanding rather than just covering the material. They become problem finders, researchers, investigators, problem solvers, and critical thinkers. Students assume more responsibility for their learning and become able to generate their own questions and solutions. Their goal is to master the content material without having to memorize it. As students become more adept with PBL, they can become self-directed and self-regulated learners. They learn to plan their work, access resources, teach their peers, and often, their teacher! In other words, students learn to initiate and manage much of their own learning, thus becoming increasingly independent and self-motivated learners.

Who chooses the problem?

The teacher chooses the problem (based on curriculum requirements) and poses the initial focus question, context for the problem, and problem parameters. After the problem is posed, the students' job is to generate what they already know about the problem, prepare a list of questions they have about the problem, and brainstorm ideas about how they might find answers. Students then choose facets of the problem to begin researching.

How often should I use problem-based learning in my curriculum?

Whenever authentic problem solving would benefit learners, and the content is suitable, the teacher may want to use PBL; how often depends on the teacher. No single teaching strategy is appropriate all the time or for all learning objectives, so teachers must use their best judgment.

PBL is especially effective for moving learning to higher levels in Bloom's taxonomy (application, analysis, synthesis, and evaluation) (Bloom, 1956). Around the world, medical schools, other professional schools, and K–12 schools use PBL as the focus for their curriculum. Teachers may choose a single PBL problem to study, develop an entire course around PBL, or use it after their students have received a general overview of relevant theories and have begun to develop a knowledge base.

Some teachers use a few PBL units at strategic times in their courses. These are often called "posthole" problems because they support the rest of the curriculum. Posthole problems may be a good way to get started with PBL.

What are some problems I might encounter?

In each chapter, the authors discuss specific problems they encountered and the potential solutions they recommend. We highlight their problems and solutions here.

Chapter 1

Problem. Large class size (40–60 students).

Solutions. Dean recommended putting students in groups, having each group study a different problem, and requiring the groups to share their problem solutions with the rest of the class. Such group-generated information can become the source for class examination questions. In addition, Dean reconfigured her class schedule so that she could take time to meet with each group to monitor their progress, answer their questions, and keep them on track. She asked school administrators to serve as resources for the groups.

Chapter 2

Problems. Handling "free riders" in group work; students' lack of awareness that logs and groups can be resources; student anxiety about essays.

Solutions. To reduce free riders in a group, Shumow recommends two ways to keep individuals accountable for their learning: periodically assessing each student's individual learning log, and giving tests regularly. She developed and shared assessment models with the students, and used rubrics to help standardize the assessment process.

Shumow suggests that teachers be very explicit about using logs and groups as resources. Students need guidance to help them realize their value.

She recommends using a directive approach to relieve student anxiety about essays. Students did not always make the connection that the rubric Shumow had given them for evaluating their essays could also guide their writing.

Chapter 3

Problems. Large amount of time needed to solve PBL problems; time and effort required of instructor; resistance from students unaccustomed to the demands of PBL.

Solutions. PBL does take a lot of time, and Pierce and Lange did not feel they could require their students to meet together outside of class. Their solutions included providing class time for groups to meet and using electronic mail for communicating with each other, the course teacher, and the classroom teacher whose children they were preparing to teach.

Pierce and Lange do not have a solution to help them address the tremendous effort that went into their work, but they believe that the authenticity of PBL is well worth their investment.

Matrices and graphic organizers provided scaffolding for students unfamiliar with self-regulated problem solving.

Chapter 4

Problems: Providing opportunities for all students to spend time in inclusion classrooms; difficulty in setting up interviews between students and itinerant professionals.

Solutions: Hibbard, Levin, and Rock arranged with Professional Development Schools to allow students to observe or spend an internship in an inclusion classroom in the schools. Sites that were not inclusion schools offered other options for helping students with disabilities, and students learned the benefits and challenges each produced.

Scheduling interviews on days when itinerant professionals are at the school site where students are observing or interning is one way to address the interviewing difficulty.

Chapter 5

Problems. Short time frame of a summer school course; varying size of groups.

Solutions. Levin adjusted the scope of the problem to the time available. Group size varied because the groups were self-selected according to common interests. Levin felt that working on a shared interest took priority over specifying a group size, so she did not change the self-selection process.

Chapter 6

Problems. Teacher confusion, frustration, and fear from struggling with trying to learn and use PBL in a short time frame (one week); making the course meaningful for all students.

Solutions. Sage offers a number of suggestions to address teacher concerns, including advising students before the workshop begins to come prepared with ideas and resources; helping teachers examine their educational beliefs to better understand PBL; creating a supportive classroom environment; and keeping the class size small, about 10–15 students.

To help make the course meaningful for students from various professional settings, she recommends providing alternative assessments in which students can describe how to apply PBL in their specific educational situation.

Chapter 7

Problems. Varying size of teams; finding enough team mentors; creating incentives for teacher participation in PBL/CAR projects.

Solutions. Originally, team size was not specified, which resulted in teams of one person or more than four. One-person teams felt overwhelmed; large teams had trouble coordinating schedules to meet and didn't always have equitable participation. To solve the problem, Mettetal required that teams have two to four educators.

Early in the program, Mettetal asked school administrators and college professors to become mentors. Over time, as a pool of mentors gradually developed, the problem of not having enough eventually solved itself.

For incentives, one district gave teachers two days' leave and paid for substitutes. Giving college credit for the course was also an incentive. Mettetal suggests seeking additional funding from federal programs and private granting agencies.

Resistance

It is possible that, in the beginning, you will encounter resistance from a variety of sources. Students may express discomfort when they realize there is no one right answer to the problem. They have been conditioned to think that only one answer exists, that the teacher has it, and that the teacher will eventually give it to them. Those who have been successful students in traditional classrooms may not like the change in teaching methods because they are afraid of failure. In fact, some students may say, "Just tell me the answer," and in college, they may say, "I'm paying you all this (tuition) money for you to *teach* me." Colleagues may not see the value in a PBL approach and view it as "soft" or "not rigorous." They believe that you cannot possibly cover all the required material. You will need to develop new, authentic assessment models because traditional multiple-choice and even essay tests are not a good match for assessing the kind of learning that can be achieved using PBL.

These areas of resistance will likely disappear (or at least moderate) with time, experience, and success with PBL. You can help new and experienced teachers understand the value of teaching to a variety of learning styles and using a variety of approaches to learning by showing them how to include PBL in their repertoire.

With well-crafted problems, teachers and students will become engaged in learning and appreciate PBL as a learning strategy.

Conclusion

We hope this book stimulates ideas for using PBL with pre-service and inservice teachers. We tried to provide examples and practical suggestions about how to organize PBL in various disciplines and types of courses, information about how to address assessment issues, and guidance about how to solve various kinds of problems that might arise when undertaking PBL for the first time. If teachers are to use PBL with their K–12 students, they themselves need guided professional development experiences with PBL. When educators hear about PBL's benefits for their students, and experience it, their response is typically, "How do I find or create problems and conduct PBL in my teaching situation?" We hope we have conveyed the value of PBL for engaging students in learning in authentic and meaningful ways as they attempt to find solutions to messy, real-world problems.

Reference

Bloom, B. S. (Ed.). (1956). *Taxonomy of educational objectives: The classification of educational goals by a committee of college and university examiners.* New York: Longmans Green.

A classic text that includes taxonomies of educational objectives in the cognitive, affective, and psychomotor domains. Bloom's taxonomy defines six levels of increasing complexity for education goals and objectives in the cognitive domain: knowledge, comprehension, application, analysis, synthesis, and evaluation.

Additional Resource

Autodesk Foundation. (2000). *About Autodesk* [Online]. Available: http://www.autodesk.com/foundation (2000, October 4).

A Web site providing a good review of project-based learning written by John Thomas.

Index

About the Authors

Carol D. Dean is an assistant professor and director of Academic Support Services and Problem-Based Learning in the Orlean Bullard Beeson (OBB) School of Education at Samford University in Birmingham, Alabama. She was a teacher in grades K–8 for 23 years before beginning her work with teacher interns and earning her doctorate in education leadership. Her research interests include factors that affect teacher quality and retention and the effects of PBL in K–12 and teacher education. At the undergraduate level, Dean teaches courses in educational foundations and language arts; at the graduate level, curriculum design and educational leadership. She designs PBL courses in teacher education at both levels. Dean can be reached at OBB School of Education and Professional Studies, Samford University, 800 Lakeshore Drive, Birmingham, AL 35229; phone: 205-726-2396; fax: 205-726-2068; e-mail: cddean@samford.edu.

Katherine L. Hibbard is an assistant professor in the Education Department at Framingham State College in Massachusetts. Her teaching interests revolve around disability and inclusion issues for general and special educators, and special education and teacher education for both undergraduate and graduate students. Her research interests include student participation in individualized education plans (IEPs), transition-service planning and self-determination; preservice teachers' attitude change and development about inclusion and disability issues; and teacher education. Hibbard can be reached at the Education Department, Framingham State College, 100 State Street, P.O. Box 9101, Framingham, MA 01701-9101; phone: 508-626-4830; e-mail: khibbard33@ hotmail.com.

Herbert G. Lange is a doctoral student at Northern Illinois University in DeKalb, where he teaches educational psychology courses. He taught secondary school for 27 years and administered a fine arts grant for four years. His research interests include problem-based learning and individual differences. Lange can be reached at 407 Timbers Circle, St. Charles, IL 60174; phone: 630-587-3090; e-mail: bltgroup@aol.com.

Barbara B. Levin is an associate professor in the Department of Curriculum and Instruction at the University of North Carolina at Greensboro (UNCG). Before earning her doctorate at the University of California-Berkeley in 1993, she was an elementary school teacher in Wisconsin for 17 years. Her research interests include the longitudinal development of teachers' pedagogical thinking, uses of case-based and problem-based learning for teacher education, and uses of technology in teacher education. At UNCG, Levin works with teams of elementary education majors in a Paideia-focused Professional Development School and teaches social studies methods to undergraduates. She also teaches elementary curriculum, educational psychology, and technology courses at the master's level; at the doctoral level, she teaches courses in cognition and motivation and in qualitative research methods. Levin can be reached at the School of Education, 345 Curry Building, P.O. Box 26171, UNCG, Greensboro, NC 27402-6171; phone: 336-334-3443; e-mail: Barbara_Levin@uncg.edu.

Gwynn Mettetal is an associate professor of educational psychology in the School of Education and director of the University

Center for Excellence in Teaching at Indiana University South Bend. She teaches courses in educational psychology, personal skills for teachers, child development, classroom management, and research methods. Mettetal's current research focus is finding ways to facilitate teacher research, and she provides support for teacher-researchers on her Web site (http://www.iusb.edu/~gmetteta). She is also a founding editor of the Web-based journal, *Journal of Scholarship of Teaching and Learning* (http://www.iusb.edu/~josotl). Mettetal can be reached at the University Center for Excellence in Teaching, Indiana University South Bend, 1700 Mishawaka Ave., South Bend, IN 46615; phone: 219-237-4507; e-mail: gmettetal@iusb.edu.

Jean W. Pierce is a professor in the Department of Educational and Psychological Foundations in the School of Education at Northern Illinois University (NIU) in DeKalb. Before earning her doctorate from Northwestern University in 1976, she taught 1st grade. Currently, she teaches learning and cognition courses in educational psychology at NIU, where she conducts research on the assessment of learner-centered practices and beliefs in higher education. Pierce can be reached at the Department of Educational and Psychological Foundations, Northern Illinois University, DeKalb, IL 60115; phone: 815-753-8470; e-mail: jpierce@niu.edu.

Tracy C. Rock is an assistant professor in the Department of Reading and Elementary Education in the College of Education at the University of North Carolina at Charlotte. Prior to earning her doctorate at the University of North Carolina at Greensboro, she was an elementary school teacher and social studies curriculum specialist. Her main teaching interests are social studies methods, teacher action research, and elementary-level curriculum. Her research interests include teacher learning from collaborative action research and teacher development in Professional Development School settings. Rock can be reached at the Department of Reading and Elementary Education, College of Education, University of North Carolina, Charlotte, NC 28223; phone: 704-547-4428; e-mail: tcrock@email.uncc.edu.

Sara M. Sage is an assistant professor of secondary education at Indiana University South Bend. She has been a special educator at the elementary and secondary levels and a professional development and research specialist for the Center for Problem-Based Learning at the Illinois Math and Science Academy. Currently, as a teacher educator, she teaches courses in problem-based learning, personal skills for teachers, general methods, individualized instruction, and principles of secondary education. Sage is coauthor of ASCD's *Problems as Possibilities: Problem-Based Learning for K–12 Education.* Her current research focuses on learners' experience in problem-based learning classes. Sage can be contacted at Indiana University South Bend, NS 376, 1700 Mishawaka Ave., South Bend, IN 46634-7111; phone: 219-237-6504; fax: 219-237-4550; e-mail: ssage@iusb.edu.

Lee Shumow is an associate professor in the Department of Educational and Psychological Foundations in the School of Education at Northern Illinois University (NIU) in DeKalb. She earned her Ph.D. from the University of Wisconsin, Madison. Shumow teaches educational psychology classes at NIU and is associated with the Social Science Research Institute. Her research is focused on sociocultural and ecological theories of learning and development. She is interested in community and family contributions to student's school adjustment as well as in teacher education. Shumow can be reached at the Department of Educational and Psychological Foundations, Northern Illinois University, DeKalb, IL 60115; phone: 815-753-8445; e-mail: Lshumow@niu.edu.

Related ASCD Resources: Problem-Based Learning

ASCD stock numbers are noted in parentheses.

Audiotapes

Problem-Based Learning (2-tape series #497172)

Problem-Based Learning Across the Curriculum
by William Stepien (#297182)

Problem-Based Learning: A Showcase for a New Vision
by Ellen Jo Ljung (#297043)

Print Products

How to Use Problem-Based Learning in the Classroom
by Robert Delisle (#197166)

Problems as Possibilities: Problem-Based Learning for K–12 Education
by Linda Torp and Sara Sage (#198010)

Problem-Based Learning Across the Curriculum
developed by William J. Stepien and Shelagh Gallagher
(ASCD Professional Inquiry Kit #997148)

Videotapes

Problem-Based Learning: Using Problems to Learn (#497172)

Problem-Based Learning: Designing Problems for Learning
(#497173)

Special Problem-Based Learning Package: two books, Professional Development Kit, and videotape (#799251)

For additional resources, visit us on the World Wide Web (http://www.ascd.org), send an e-mail message to member@ascd.org, call the ASCD Service Center (1-800-933-ASCD or 703-578-9600, then press 2), send a fax to 703-575-5400, or write to Information Services, ASCD, 1703 N. Beauregard St., Alexandria, VA 22311-1714 USA.